MY WITHERED LEGS
AND OTHER ESSAYS

Series editor

NICOLE WALKER

Series advisory board

STEVE FELLNER

KIESE LAYMON

LIA PURPURA

PAISLEY REKDAL

WENDY S. WALTERS

ELISSA WASHUTA

MY WITHERED LEGS AND OTHER ESSAYS

SANDRA GAIL LAMBERT

Sandra Gail Lambert

THE UNIVERSITY OF GEORGIA PRESS ATHENS

Published by the University of Georgia Press
Athens, Georgia 30602
www.ugapress.org
© 2024 by Sandra Gail Lambert
All rights reserved
Designed by Kaelin Chappell Broaddus
Set in 11/13.5 Kepler Std Regular by Kaelin Chappell Broaddus
Printed and bound by Sheridan Books, Inc.
The paper in this book meets the guidelines for permanence
and durability of the Committee on Production Guidelines for
Book Longevity of the Council on Library Resources.

Most University of Georgia Press titles are
available from popular e-book vendors.

Printed in the United States of America
28 27 26 25 24 P 5 4 3 2 1

Library of Congress Cataloging-in-Publication Data

Names: Lambert, Sandra Gail, author.
Title: My withered legs and other essays / Sandra Gail Lambert.
Description: Athens : The University of Georgia Press, [2023] |
    Series: Crux, the Georgia series in literary nonfiction
Identifiers: LCCN 2023024906 | ISBN 9780820365909 (paperback) |
    ISBN 9780820365916 (epub) | ISBN 9780820365923 (pdf)
Subjects: LCSH: Lambert, Sandra Gail. | Women authors, American—
    Biography.
Classification: LCC PS3612.A54648 Z46 2023 | DDC 813/.6—dc23/eng/20230628
LC record available at https://lccn.loc.gov/2023024906

CONTENTS

MY WITHERED LEGS AND OTHER ESSAYS

OLD POLIO

The bus step was at waist level. I was ten years old. The bus driver stood beside me with her hand at the small of my back. But not touching. It wouldn't count if she touched. She had been lifting and pushing me up the steps, but now the school principal said she wasn't allowed to touch. And since I couldn't get up the bus steps by myself, the principal said I'd have to go to the school for handicapped kids. I'd overheard my parents talking about it. We were freshly arrived in Virginia and not living on a military base because my father was assigned to the Pentagon, which I now understand meant I was one of the few military kids at the school. So my parents didn't have the support of a base community or the federal government. Or maybe they'd had to push back before, but this was the first time I was old enough to realize it. The principal told them they already had one of us, a blind girl, and didn't want to deal with another.

I like to remember the bus driver as having a body that strained against her clothes and a cigarette-gruff voice. It's possible she smoked on the bus. These days, of course, that is unimaginable. It would also be unimaginable that a bus driver would take it on herself, just her and me, without my parents knowing, without the school knowing, to have me stay on the bus until everyone else was gone and teach me to climb the steps. She had pulled into a parking lot and snapped the doors open. Using my controlled fall technique, I threw myself down the steps with more abandon than usual. This was an adventure. She came and stood beside me. We stared up at the steps. How could I climb them and climb them without showing my panties? Dress wearing was mandatory.

She pointed out the long silver pole along one side for me to grab on to. She said, you're strong, right? I was strong. I'd walked with crutches from the beginning, since I could walk, since I was two. So as her hand moved behind my back, not touching, I slid one crutch so it dangled from my forearm before I grabbed the pole as high up as I could. My fingers were short and chubby the way they still are. They couldn't close around the pole, but I had a hardened grip. I'd long been the jar opener of the family. My weight rammed back onto my other arm and down the crutch wrapped around it. The wide rubber tip locked into a well of gravel and dirt. I bounced a little to make sure it was secure, which I knew to do from walking in snow during our last posting in Norway.

On our return from overseas, as usual, we had an appointment for new braces at the orthotics department of the Warm Springs Polio Foundation. This time they had fitted me with an ankle-height metal bar that attached my legs together with my toes pointed forward. It was another attempt to straighten my tibias. It was annoying in the way it limited movement. But on this day I figured out that if I kept the knee locks in place and twisted sideways, I could use my relatively stronger side to swing both legs between my suspended body, together, straight out, back and forth, until I had enough momentum to flip them up on the first step. So now I was bent ninety degrees at the waist. Cool air reached up my thighs, but my skirt hung low, almost to the ground. I could sense the bus driver's hand wavering. I flexed the arm holding on to the pole. I concentrated. At first nothing happened, but then effort overcame gravity, and I rose and unfolded until the weight came off my back arm, the crutch rose into the air, and I was standing upright on the first step. Best I could tell, there hadn't been a glimpse of underpants.

It was nothing to hop up the next two steps. I twirled around in place and the bus driver had both arms raised to celebrate our shared triumph. She drove me back to my regular bus stop, and I walked home and told my mother I could now get on the bus by myself. My shoulder never hurt that I remember, but I wouldn't have noticed.

The blind girl was older than I was. Unlike me, she was tall. Also unlike me, she claimed the space around her with both her posture and a cane. When she passed by, I stopped moving and pressed close to the wall. I didn't want her to be alerted by the clang of the crutches or the rattle of the buckles that strapped the braces to my legs. I didn't want her to know I was there. I didn't want her to talk to me. We were competitors for the small space permitted the handi-capped. Ten-year-old me had no concern for kids with dis-abilities who weren't strong in the same way I was, a way that made the bus steps possible, barely. All my childhood there was fear about dropping below the barely.

In 1973 the Rehabilitation Act with its Section 504 man-dated full inclusion in public education, transportation, and housing for anywhere receiving federal funds. Two years later the Education for All Handicapped Children Act passed. New regulations on the books didn't change much until disabled people used the new laws to protest and sue. But all this was after I'd finished college.

When I went to college, there was one handmade hand-icapped sign attached to a tree in front of one parking place. I had wanted to escape the strictures of dorm life that were still true for women in the 1970s, so I manipu-lated my way through parental objections until I had an off-campus apartment where I could drink too much, use drugs, and have ill-advised sexual partners. One day, when

I was hungover and late to class, I parked in that hand-icapped parking place. I got a ticket. I took my crutches-and braces-using self to the windowless basement offices where you paid your tickets and stated the obvious. I was handicapped, and so I used the handicapped space. I tilted my head. My voice was all innocence. A woman, cloaked in parking enforcement authority, said that space was for one specific faculty member and no one else. The hint of trag-edy in her voice made me think this person was either ter-minal or newly injured. Those of us with long-term disabil-ity or chronic illness didn't elicit that support. I did not pull the checkbook out of my purse. I tilted my head to the other side, shifted one braced leg behind the other, and leaned on my crutches. I might have had a ponytail flipped over one shoulder.

It was a stare-off. I won. She asked for the exact hours of my classes and gave me a sticker that let me park on cam-pus, but, she warned, just in a few places and just for those times exactly. And not in that handicapped space. I almost pushed for library time or even enough leeway to walk to and from class, but I had already insulted her author-ity. And the sticker indicated it was restricted parking but didn't say how. Every time I parked I got a ticket, and every time I called the department and they voided it. When I was challenged on the times, I said I had new classes. What did they want me to do? They got tired of my calls, and the tick-ets stopped. And that's when I started parking wherever I wanted to, for as long as I wanted. If you were four foot ten, sweet faced, white, quietly bull-headed, and at an expensive private college (on scholarship, but in the parking depart-ment they didn't know that), you could sometimes expand someone else's individual solution to become your own. It made a basic need of my education possible.

I'm what's called an "old polio." We are called that, some-times as a simple fact, sometimes in a denigrating way, sometimes for good reason, by the post–American with

Disabilities Act generation of disability rights activists. As a group we old polios were integrated back into society perhaps more than any other group of modern-day disabled people ever have been. We have high levels of employment, of education, and of marriage. But the unspoken deal was that in return we would never complain or ask for anything. We were known as the John Waynes of disability and proud of it. John Waynes not in the racist, misogynist way (not that we weren't) but that we were stoic and we were perfectionists. Succeeding no matter what became part of my sense of self. The harder something was, the more accomplished I felt. There was no worse insult than calling me lazy. The language of civil rights was unknown and incomprehensible to me. My language had whispered angry words—"get out of my way, just try to stop me, shut up, you won't win, I can outlast you."

The best I remember, the culture of women's self-care began in the 1980s. In my feminist bookstore, our bestsellers included many self-help titles that emphasized women putting themselves first. It was now the feminist thing to do. Part-timers would call at the last minute to say they weren't coming in because they needed to take care of themselves that day. I understood, didn't I? I didn't. I couldn't imagine making a call like that. And it meant that I, who had come in at five because I thought I'd have relief later, had to work thirteen hours that day, had to unpack box after box of books and carry them to the shelves, had no way to get lunch, and had to risk the cash register being left alone to rush to the bathroom. Midday, nine hours in, a customer put *Women Who Love Too Much, Codependent No More,* and *The Road Less Traveled* on the counter. I did not visibly sneer. I did ring up the large sale and was glad for the money to help pay off the bills due that week.

Those young, abled women who cancelled at the last moment were praised for some sort of reclaiming of personal power. I knew if I behaved in a similar manner, it would be because I was disabled and disabled people can't be counted on to do their job and the problem with hiring us was when we (inevitably, was the general consensus) didn't do our job, it was awkward to fire us. So it didn't matter that I was the boss, I still showed up, always early, and got it done.

In 1990, when I was thirty-eight, two years after I traded in crutches for a wheelchair, the Americans with Disabilities Act was signed into law. For the first time we had civil rights, and discrimination against us was illegal. The enforcement of it was again slow, focused on physical barriers, driven by lawsuits and civil disobedience actions, and continues today more than thirty years later. But mostly I can get in places and no longer have to plan my day around where I'm going to pee. Unless it's an airplane or a private home.

More than a generation of people in the United States have been born into a world where, at least on paper, disabled people have rights. The younger me would have felt a stranger in this universe where common words, even slurs, now had meanings that were legal or specific or positive: "damages," "path of travel," "distance learning," "crip politics," "access is love," "undue burden," and even what it means to work. I don't remember what decade it was when instead of asking "Can I get in?" I used the word "accessible." I don't remember when I realized that was a narrow interpretation of the word. Disability rights activists would rant about accommodations versus accessibility. It took me a while, but when I understood the difference, layers of my life fell into a structural order. The parking enforcement woman accommodated me (barely). The situation was inaccessible. The last of the "ugly laws" that allowed for the removal and arrest of "the deformed" from the streets were repealed in the 1970s. They had stopped being widely enforced decades earlier, and I had no direct knowledge of them growing up except that I knew my presence was on sufferance. Their legacy is part of the atmosphere I breath in and move through even as I sometimes name myself, with pride, a crip.

A pre-COVID writers' conference has multiple sessions in multiple time slots, and I've overbooked myself for many of them. But my priority is the one that includes a young disabled writer who creates wildly imaginative multimedia pieces. The work is so different from mine—something I think I could never do. But it already inspires me to be less linear, less careful, more intuitive. The time comes and it's afternoon, I'm beyond tired, and a solitary hotel room with a luxurious bed is just across the street. One more, just this one more event, I promise myself. It'll be worth it. At the door to the meeting room, a friend is already leaving. The writer we had both wanted to meet has been unable to travel.

The writer was going appear via video instead but cancelled that as well when one of the conference's organizers said something about how a remote presentation was a lesser form of participation. "But they weren't disallowing it, right?" I ask my friend. They weren't. And then, even in my fatigue, I'm angry. Not at the organizers but at the writer. Why should she let herself be silenced by a little kickback, a snarky comment? It was still possible to be there. Who mattered most, other disabled writers who supported her work or some administrative drone of an ignorant, ableist conference employee who had no ongoing say in her life and no power over her physically, financially, medically, or career-wise? I heard myself spitting out one of the right wing's current favorite epitaphs: "Fucking snowflake."

Back at Warm Springs there was a room, the cast room, where stretchers filled the space. Tough men moved among them with buzzing saws. The saws were run up the sides of legs and backs, and screeched as they cut through plaster. Sometimes the saws would nick into spongy skin damp from weeks or months under a cast. White dust spread the smell of chalk and motor oil throughout the room and mixed with the screams of little children. Not all the children cried. I don't remember which I was. Either way, this might have been where I learned that crying got you nowhere. Another old polio tells me she remembers that room as well and knows she never cried. She remembers calling the screamers the worst word her five-year-old self knew. They were nothing but "babies." Babies or snowflakes, the scorn is the same.

This young, brilliant, creative writer told the conference no, I withdraw, you don't get to have me here. I questioned, and still question, her choice. What about the importance of using your work to give other disabled people the chance to explore what is possible and to build community? And the John Wayne me thought there was an element of grandstanding, and what did she want, anyway, the red-carpet treatment or some sort of mythical "safe space"? But the refusal to appear and subsequent public uproar led to a reevaluation of attitudes and restrictions about video presentations in a way her showing up never would have. A few years later, of course, the entire conference was online.

At Warm Springs they made the doors harder to open than they were anywhere else in order to "prepare" us. It was boot camp mentality, and I thrived on it. Recently, I was at a university and pressed a push plate to open the door. It didn't work. I smacked it again, this time with the side of my fist. And then again. By now my elbow ached. People around me stared. Some offered the advice that I should report it. One person did open the door and hold it for me. I said thank you as I went through, but it annoyed me that I forgot for a moment I was still capable of opening a door on my own. And if I'd just done that from the get-go, my arm would hurt less and I'd already be where I was going.

Over and over modern-day disability activists say, "If it's hard, something is wrong." Over and over I've internally responded, "You wuss, that's not the point. Can you accomplish what you want to accomplish or not? Fuck them and figure it out." My resilience, the dignity I find in endurance, my adamant belief that help is fine but to always make sure you can do it on your own, and the parameters of my physical ability that have allowed this belief—these lifelong survival skills have not lent themselves to flexibility or to compassion.

So back to doors. I was at another writer's conference working on personal essays, some of them about my childhood. The doors to the outside patio where we ate were heavy and full-length glass, which is a bad combination for me in my power chair while holding a plate of food in one hand. I mean, I can do it, but it's risky. One day I thought, "This really shouldn't be so hard." And then I thought it again. "No, I mean really. This shouldn't be so hard."

Holding that plate of ziti with chicken and pesto with my wrist starting to shake from the weight of it, I considered my life. What would have happened if so much hadn't been so hard? If I hadn't been chronically scared about the consequences of the barely possible becoming impossible? And these days, at seventy, many things waver on that border— lifting up out of the bathtub, pain that prevents sleeping, exhaustion that limits my writing, remembering words, those damn doors in front of me. I backed away, turned, found a staff person, and asked them to open the door for me. I did this for the rest of the conference . . . mostly, not always.

What if it hadn't been so hard? I wake with the question in my mind. My fingers type it into whatever essay I'm working on as its own paragraph with spacing above and below. Almost a year after eating that ziti, I think, "Just answer the question." What if? Would I have spoken to the blind girl? We wouldn't have been friends because she was two grades above me, which is a chasm of time at that age. But we would have known each other was there.

Pulling up the bus steps wasn't the first or last of ways my body was pushed to its limits. One college semester I had classes at opposite ends of campus and ten minutes between them. I can still feel the ball rotating in my shoulder socket as I threw myself through my crutches as far and fast as I could and still arrived late, red faced, and layered in sweat. I missed announcements about dates of exams and new assignments. Today, in both arms, that ball and socket catch and click against each other when I transfer into my bed. A more accessible world would have given me more years of less pain.

It's harder to consider the parts that aren't physical. In this imagining of growing up in a world that wasn't so hard, what would success mean? What would I consider an accomplishment? How would I triumph? Would I even want to triumph? I'd have to be a different person for this not to seem like a loss. There's all sorts of bad logic to this speculation. I was the oldest child, and our household was heavy on focus and discipline, so with or without a disability, I might have been a child who strived.

The poet Naomi Ortiz wrote a self-help book. It's about self-care for disability activists, among others. My first exposure to writing about disability included work by Nancy Mairs. Her subject matter was sometimes similar to Ortiz's, but Mairs consistently wrote to an abled audience, which, no matter how insightful her essays, left me excluded and lonely and angry. I've been able to read Ortiz's book in pieces and from time to time. The words are written to me, but the past endures and I'm wary. Still, sometimes a passage creates a wash of generosity and kindness that makes me touch into the depression at the bottom of my neck, the jugular notch. The words and the touch leave me uncomfortable. And comforted.

I watch wheelchair motocross videos. There's fourteen-year-old Lily Rice flying up into the air and flipping her neon green wheelchair into a twisty somersault. At fourteen, in 1966, I was technically physically capable of being strapped into a manual wheelchair and pushing myself off a concrete ledge. Except I wouldn't have. Besides the fact that

BMX hadn't been imagined yet, even the camera shot of her inverted angle of descent makes me sweat. But when I was fourteen I lived in Norway. I had a wooden sled capable of a wonderfully terrifying level of speed, but if I was fourteen today, perhaps I would be a sit-ski giant slalom Paralympic contender. Right now, as I'm writing this, a friend, a Paralympic athlete, is at a Disabled Veterans Winter Sports Clinic learning to ski for the first time. She's in her sixties. I google "adaptive skiing." If you have enough money, there are all sorts of classes. But after a short time of excited clicking through sites, I start the list: The cold hurts my joints. I can't risk an injury to my arms. I am not fourteen. Would I even enjoy it? The skier is tethered to a guy behind her, so you're not really on your own. That would annoy me. All that money and effort for a just a day or two of fun that can't be recreated when I get home to Florida. I close down the research tabs. Instead, as usual, I return to a relentless focus on what is possible. I research snorkeling excursions. As far as I can tell, they involve lying on my stomach and dog paddling. It would be fun and exciting and also warm. Still, there is grief. I grew up surrounded by mountains and slopes in the place where skiing was invented, and I was young and strong. I was right there. The time was wrong.

I open a video of Erin Clark. She scoots to the edge of the cushion in her manual wheelchair. She reaches as high up on the pole as she can. In a way that seems lacking in gravity, her body is out of the chair. It happens so quickly that I rewind the video to understand where she puts her hands. When I restart it, she is upside down with her legs ninety degrees sideways, and she makes quick circles around the pole. I rewind again and try to understand the physics of her momentum by shadowing her movements with my own arms. Then she is upright with one hand gripped over her head and the other tucked into the small of her own back, the pole secured in her armpit. She can wrap her legs around the pole, which I couldn't have. I imagine wrapping my legs together in shiny teal silks. I'd have been the mermaid pole dancer. My arms are shorter than Erin's, but when I was in my late twenties, my arms might have been stronger than hers.

In my youth I could have done a version of this physically, but then it was unimaginable. In contrast to learning to ski which is still possible, the absolute impossibility of lifting my body high into the air makes it easier to lose myself in the daydream of twirling around that pole. Erin wears black bike shorts and a halter top. She explores the performance art of pole dancing. She competes in it as a sport. She inhabits her body in a sensuous, athletic way.

But for most of my life "working the pole" meant erotic dancing in strip clubs. As I conjure my performance in my imagined, fantastical universe, I hear pounding music. This is going to be fun. I've had large breasts since I was eleven. They offer a wide surface to bedazzle with glitter and rhinestones. When I bend my body backward to grab the pole, the splatter of reflections from my bra lights the room. And there is fringe as well. Fringe that falls from my hips so my thighs are seen and then not seen. And each time I flip upside down, my panties show.

RELATIONSHIP TIPS

Before our first date, Pam searches the Internet for "how to date someone in a wheelchair." I don't know this. All I know before our first date is that for years my mostly coupled friends suggest her to me as girlfriend material. Whenever Pam and I were single at the same time, one of the couples would say—in that particular choral pattern that couples have, not quite in unison, but overlapping over the ends of each other's sentences—that I should check her out. The investment my friends have in ending my years of aloneness is greater than mine, but I did check her out. Pam is a cutie. At a concert, I said hi. She was minimally polite in return. A few years later she was at a restaurant with a group I knew. I stopped by their table to say hello. Everyone greeted me except Pam. A few years after that, at a Pride Center reception, I came alongside her in the buffet line and made a comment about the brownies. How many times she could ignore me had become my own private game. This time she looked over my head and said nothing. I'm done, I thought. The game isn't fun anymore. My life as a single person continued.

Once a well-meaning (able-bodied) friend suggested a dating strategy: Ask out three women, any three. No big deal. Maybe one will say no, but humiliation is part of dating. But chances are you'll get two coffee dates. One will be tedious. What's the harm? At least you'll have a story to tell us. (Did this last part of the instructions imply she thought my life was boring?) My dating instructor was right about the inevitable humiliation. All three of the women I awkwardly asked out had the same panicked, twirly-eyed look when they turned me down.

I was in my sixties when Pam joined Facebook. She "liked" all my posts. She said nice things about my dog, my writing, my camping trips. In return I "liked" her posts about training for a marathon. She seemed to be fond of classic jazz standards. I learned she plays piano. Later, after we are dating, Pam will say she didn't understand Facebook yet and had no idea what all that liking implied. But before our first date, I don't know that she doesn't know how to use Facebook. I do know she still has those sleepy eyes and octave-spanning hands. Her "likings" have made me bold. I put aside the previous rejections and try again. This time I don't mess around with coffee. I don't want anything that allows for a graceful out into friendship. I ask her on a date, a dinner date.

Soon after I came out, a woman I was dating, who used a wheelchair, made gingerbread lesbians for all her friends as Christmas presents. They had chocolate chip breasts and curled chocolate shavings between the legs. She pressed one red sprinkle down into the curls to represent a clitoris. (It was the 1970s, and we all still had lovely bushes of pubic hair.)

She asked if I would help deliver the treats. I still used braces and crutches then, and it was possible for me to get up the steps to someone's door. My job was to knock and ask whoever answered to come out to the woman who I was dating's car so she could give them the festive plates.

I was new in town and therefore unknown in her lesbian community. I'd knock and give the spiel, but most of them fidgeted with the door handle, stepped back, and didn't seem to hear anything I said. Sometimes they would say no thank you and shut the door in my face. This is where I first noticed that twirly-eyed panic. I went back to the car and reported the situation. After the second time, we figured it out. All they saw was a handicapped person at their door at Christmastime. No matter what I said, no matter that I used their good friend's name to introduce myself, I could only be someone asking for a donation or a handout.

The waitstaff is distracted, and the food is abysmal. I'm nauseated from new medications and have to grip my armrests and hope I don't vomit. Besides that, my standard dating terror has transformed me into a robot version of myself. Pam is charming. I'm so sad at the end, because I couldn't carry off the ninety minutes of not being weird required by a first date. I tried. I failed. There's a relief to that. But later Pam calls me. Even later she says she'd considered the date a bust except for a moment at the end. I don't know what changed, but she'd thought, "There she is."

My little dog, Pippin, is a rescue. I saw her listed on one of those matchmaking sites for dogs. She's a terrier mix, which I found out means she wakes up every morning with a plan to dominate the world—or at least me. My job has been to take enough of an edge off to allow us a pleasant life together and to keep her safe around a four-hundred-pound wheelchair. Pippin and I went to classes that taught us how to communicate with each other. She learned to sit, lay down, and "leave it." She learned to walk beside me and, if not heel, at least not run in front of my wheels. Keeping her out of the kitchen while I moved around in that small space took longer. I learned that she knows what I mean when I ask her to come but is unlikely to do so. But she never runs away. I learned she considers chicken bones found by the side of the road exempt from the "leave it" command. But she does tolerate my two-finger grab into her mouth to pull out decayed, discarded Popeyes' lunch leavings. Mostly we have learned to be patient with each other.

After our third date, I report back to friends that I want to marry Pam. Although how I say it is, "Not marry marry, of course. But have that type of relationship." I say it that way because despite the scattered places it's allowed, marriage doesn't yet seem real legally and has never been real to me in all the other ways. Friends are shocked. I knew they would be. They know me to be someone appalled that lesbians' focus of resistance has shifted from fighting the patriarchy and racism to something as status quo as marriage. Yet I want to be married to Pam and not in a so-I-can-get-health-insurance way. I want it in that other way I know so little about. But I want it. I don't tell Pam this. Not yet.

Once I was asked if, as a child, I ever imagined my future partner or family. I hadn't. Ever. I asked if this was something kids did. Yes, the woman asking me said. Her voice was sad. Her sadness made me uncomfortable.

Pam and I have our first sex talk. I say many words about the long periods of physical aloneness in my life from childhood hospitalizations to now, and how this last stretch of aloneness has included a decade of passion-killing menopausal sleeplessness and anxiety, which has only recently lessened. I say that, when she kisses me, I feel desire, but as if from a far distance. But I desire to have desire. I stop talking, sure I've failed in my explanation. I've arrived at her house just as she was back from a morning run. We've fallen into this conversation before she can take a shower, so she goes to do that now.

After a minute, Pam comes back out into the living room, naked, and asks if I would like to watch her shower. I follow her down the hall. I've never seen her naked before. Desire becomes less distant. During the shower, water drips and beads and runs down her body in all the ways we've all seen in all the sex scenes of movies. She smiles at me from time to time, but mostly goes about the business of a shower. This isn't about sex. Well, it is about sex, but it is also a wordless response to all my words, a communication of understanding and of willingness.

This is my first "take me, take my dog" relationship. Despite all her liking of my dog posts, Pam doesn't know much about dogs. She makes the effort to learn. I referee some. I direct the little dog to her crate, and tell Pam that the snatching of food off her plate and the ignoring of "No, no" wasn't personal. But really, it is. Pippin is thrilled with the new opportunities for dominance and has judged Pam as an easy mark. I advise Pam about consistency and that anger is neither productive nor allowed.

Pam and I have a fight. We are waiting at the end of my driveway to cross the road. It's a quiet neighborhood, and the only car in sight pulls to an alarmed stop just short of us. The woman behind the wheel waves in a frantic way for me to cross in front of her. I don't move. I look away until she gives up and continues on. Pam asks why I acted that way. I say the woman was treating me as if I were a toddler who might dart out in front of her. Pam asks how can I possibly know that. It seems to her the woman was just being considerate. My voice rises. I say that I'm the one with experience. I know what I'm talking about. Who was she not to believe me? Pam says I don't get to say what she should or shouldn't think. She says I can be too "directive." I've heard this before. I know it means bossy and controlling. I say disabled people have to be very, very clear. We have to say spe-

cifically what we want, need, and perceive to be happening;
that my control makes my life possible. Pam says she gets
to come to things in her own way. We have no resolution.

Visibly disabled people are often asked questions. How do
you take a shower? (Soap and water.) Tell me about the
hydraulics on your lift van. (I don't know what hydraulics
are.) How fast does that wheelchair go? (Vacant smile as I
keep going past the heckler.) Can you have sex? (Fuck off.)
How do you use the toilet? (Fuck off so much.) Where can
I get my grandma a chair like yours? (Here's the number
for my wheelchair place. They'll take you through the pro-
cess. Does she have Medicare? If not, you can also get some
good deals off of Craig's list. People who died, you know. But
whatever.) It is always my pleasure to help old people be
mobile. But ever since the Internet became ubiquitous, I've
wondered why people don't just look for answers on their
own rather than use me as their encyclopedia of disability.

It's a year into our relationship when someone asks us how
we met, and I find out why Pam had been dismissive of me
in the past. I have never asked. I don't know if she remembers or noticed. In her forthright way she tells this friend
that she'd always liked me but had been scared. Because of
my wheelchair. I hold my breath. We plan to move in together, which I see as progress toward my still unspoken to
her getting-married plan. I don't want what she says next to
ruin it. I don't want to find that, somehow, I haven't noticed
she's an ableist piece of shit who harbors creepy caretaking
fantasies or pity or has some autonomy-diminishing perception of our relationship. I also don't want to hear anything about how she doesn't notice I'm disabled. (I do, even
in that moment, realize that I'm not leaving much room for
her to get it right.) That's when I find out she looked it up
on the Internet—how to date someone in a wheelchair. I've

never looked it up myself. I wait to hear what Pam found. The Internet told her to not assume I will stay in my wheelchair at the table and not to assume I won't. To ask before helping. To listen to the answer. That if the staff asks her what I want, to redirect them. To at all costs avoid saying, "Wanna race?" To not worry about being perfect. She says the permission to make mistakes helped the most. I am relieved. My marriage plan can continue.

Pippin figures out that having Pam around works to her advantage. They go on runs together. Pam gives her treats after every walk, whereas I have always thought the walk itself was the reward. The crook of Pam's knees is more cave-like and warmer to sleep in. They work out their own routines and limits. The little dog is different with Pam. When I cry, she becomes anxious and barks at me. With Pam she rests her chin on Pam's knee to comfort her. When they walk the neighborhood streets together, she doesn't snark at other dogs the way she does with me (except for the fluffy brown dog in the house across from the park, who is her archenemy). Pam and I decide that the little dog doesn't think Pam protection is in her job description and that any emotional instability on her (Pam's) part will not significantly affect her (the dog's) routine. And when all three of us stroll together and Pam has the leash, the little dog's damn nose stays millimeters from Pam's calf in a perfect heel. Pam has never asked her to do this. This is the arena where she (the dog) and I have most often tried to make the other do what we want.

It's become a joke between us (me and the dog). When she forgets herself and pulls in front of Pam, she will self-correct back into that perfect heel position. Then she gives me a sly glance of triumph just in case I had ever for a second thought she didn't understand what I wanted from her. I mutter, "You bitch." We share a laugh (me and the dog).

Which means I shake my head and roll my eyes, while she snorts and gives me side eye. Dog humor is often about winning a power play.

Growing up lesbian and disabled in the 1950s and 1960s had left me not only without the words but also lacking an imagination about the coupled state. From the first, men seemed like another species. Not bad necessarily, but rather biologically and emotionally incompatible. They confused me. I figure that was the lesbian part mostly. Never being included in make-believe weddings or given baby dolls to care for or asked coy questions about boys by adults or my peers, that was about disability. This exclusion from the cultural universal of relationships had left me ignorant and awkward. It did, of course, have benefits in that I grew up without expected roles.

Since I grew up sort of a separate species, I decide to follow Pam's example. I study human relationships. I read scholarly articles about how the lack of role models for people with disabilities allows altered thinking. I read about how some children who are deaf, who have never known a deaf or hard-of-hearing adult, believe they will become hearing at a certain age, while others believe they will die young. Those are the choices their imaginations allow. My best resource turns out to be the websites that offer 10, 25, 101 relationships tips. The sites are silly, and the ads gum up my computer, but I learn about love languages. I learn concepts like compassion, forgiveness, and presence. And it seems that "compromise" has a meaning besides lowering one's standards or becoming untrustworthy.

Pippin and I don't fuss with each other much these days. Sometimes I enforce rules, but she starts it. She lies on the bedspread but slips her chin over onto the not-allowed sheets and makes eyes at me until I notice and say "SHEETS" at her. She moves her head back and smirks. As usual, the trainer/trainee roles are blurred. Sometimes she puts the tips of her front paws over the threshold into the kitchen while I'm scooping up her dinner. She just wants me to say "Get out of here!" But I have to say it in a poorly rendered New York accent or she won't pull her paws back. We love Pam together. When Pam arrives at the door, the little dog executes a series of exuberant, gravity-scoffing leaps with more twirls than an Olympic skater. I whoop along with her.

Pam is going to move in. I worry that I'll be too . . . well, me, and micromanage the endeavor to such a degree that she bolts. But I am a good planner. I have the skills. I make timelines and lists of chores for the move, but I keep them private. I tell myself that they are there if Pam asks. Deciding it will be suspicious if I don't take charge of something, I decide on the piano. Wherever the piano goes, Pam will follow is what I tell myself. I ask Pam if I can handle this particular detail. She agrees. I hire a piano mover. I set a date. I push furniture this way and that and measure spaces. The piano arrives without mishap and slips into the allotted spot as planned and the house is changed. It expands. It's as if Pam is here. And I was right. She does follow the piano. And when she plays Pippin comes from wherever she is to lie on the couch, as close to the piano bench as possible. She puts her chin on her paw and listens. Every time. For all the years that follow.

MY WITHERED LEGS (WHAT IS LOST)

Early on in my writing life, which for me was in my forties, I wrote a thinly-disguised-as-fiction piece about a woman who needed to make immense changes in her life and how was she going to have enough courage to live into the consequences. The story explored themes of independence and isolation, of disability and desire. The woman used a wheelchair. She was a lesbian.

It was unusual for me to have feedback from what I thought of as "real" writers. And as I was becoming more serious about writing, this lack of access to knowledge was exasperating. It seemed impossible to make what I wanted to say work on the page. I'd read Dorothy Allison and yearned to write dialogue as effectively. How did Alice Walker structure a story like that? I wanted to twist the reader's brain like Joanna Russ. And *Beloved*—it was absurd to think I could ever lift my writing into such rarefied layers of the atmosphere. But I wanted to try. The next move, it seemed to me, was that I had to show my work to people outside of my friendly hometown lesbian writers' groups. A writer I knew who was a college professor and had actually been published said she would take a look at my story.

This college professor read my piece and told me having a character disabled and a lesbian was too messy, too complex for a short story. She thought that since there was no tension or plot development about being a lesbian, I should leave that part out. And here it was, right during my first foray into a wider (straight) writing world—lesbian erasure. My lesbian-feminist self was outraged. I thought, "Not enough lesbian content, I'll show you lesbian content." So I added a part about my character noticing the hands of a waitress at Shoney's. How strong the fingers were. How competently they handled the heavy plates. The way her thumb gripped into the sweaty glass of ice water. My character made a joke about the waitress' sensible shoes. I dyked up that story all over the place. I even gave my character a Barbara Stanwyck obsession and had her fantasize about the thick black leather belt Victoria Barkley, power femme personified, wore cinched above her jodhpurs on "Big Valley."

My story became one of those crowd-pleasers. I'd read it at gatherings and get all sorts of laughs and accolades, and I liked that. I didn't like that my double down defensive reaction to the feedback meant the original story had been derailed. Disability and desire were still there. The exploration of independence versus isolation was gone. Each time I read the story, amid the applause, I mourned. And I knew right then, back then, that there was the loss of something as yet unknown to me.

I kept searching out places and people who would teach me. I had very little money and my energy was limited. I audited a fiction writing class at our community college. I discovered the world of writing residencies and conferences. Some offered scholarships and sometimes I stole from my savings account to pay the fees. It was at these residencies and conferences where I learned about literary journals and that you could submit your work to them and that my writing was considered literary.

The first time I ever received a personalized rejection, the editors of the journal included a full page of feedback about my short story (another thinly-disguised-as-fiction piece). They thought I might find it helpful. I was thrilled. I'd almost been published. And I'd received a rejection notice with handwriting on it. This was the first time I'd ever seen so many words written about my writing.

> The writer skips over too many places in the story that seemed to ask for more when a woman is dealing with life from the vantage point of a wheelchair. . . . What about useless legs trailing behind her as she swam? Maybe there is the bigger point here that a person without the use of her legs doesn't focus on these things, but even if she doesn't focus on these things, *for some reason* [italics added] I have to see them.

What did he want? Was my character, a woman successfully paddling by herself deep in the Florida backcountry, supposed to have a self-hating monologue about her body in order to satisfy some unnamed, highly suspect need in the editor? It's not as if I hadn't known since childhood about the dissonance between my reality and what other people thought and assumed about me. But this was the first time I'd been told so clearly that my take on my own life wasn't enough, wasn't valid, wasn't publishable. The thought of bridging that chasm by pandering to prejudiced notions of disability disgusted me. At the same time, I wasn't willing to be kept from the education and chance to improve that comes from submitting work out into the world. And once I'd finished—way too many months later—ranting about the terrible wrongness of that feedback, I reread it. This time I noticed another paragraph. In it he wrote about how I didn't give enough attention to making each scene work toward a central theme. There it was—the next skill, the next understanding I needed. I took that sentence of feedback and used it to jump my writing forward.

And this is how I continued. At a workshop, other writers were shocked that I didn't "reveal" that my character used a wheelchair until three paragraphs in. (Which was when it naturally appeared in context.) They complained they felt tricked because an important, central detail had been left out. One of them literally sputtered, spit flying over our papers. It was as if I was supposed to announce the wheelchair in the first phrase of the first sentence. But at that same workshop another writer showed me how to make a chart to keep track of my submissions to journals. I still use it. And another taught me about nuance in introducing characters.

When I finally dropped the veil of fiction and started writing personal essays, people were somewhat less likely to tell me I was wrong about my own life. (And the fiction I did write became stronger.) Although there's an assumption that everyone under a certain age who uses a wheelchair must have had a spinal cord injury. Readers, editors, and even the staff in doctors' offices have argued with me that I don't have feeling in my legs. Really. I had polio. I have feeling. Fortunately, sort of, as I age there are other assumptions about why I use a wheelchair—general decrepitude, for instance.

The obsession with my legs continues. No matter what the theme of my essay or story—lesbian love, wilderness exploration, mother/daughter relationships—it seems everyone wants me to include more or at least something about how I feel about my legs. I've never understood that. Why would I think about my legs all the time? Okay, sometimes my legs are a part of the story, so a legitimate point can be made that I should write more about them. But then the next sentence of the critique will offer up examples of how I can do that. "Useless" continues to be a frequent descriptor offered. Other choices have included "atrophied," "flabby," and "withered."

I'm a regular person. I have bad hair days and nothing-fits-right days and this-bra-makes-me-bulge-in-weird-places days and when-did-I-get-that-new-age-spot days.

And I've had bad leg days as well that have never once involved the words "withered" or "useless." My bad leg days are more about how my foot puffs up above the line of my shoe, and my socks persist in wrinkling around my ankles.

It helps that I had some extra decades of living before my writing was read by anyone. This added emotional steadiness offers perspective, but not necessarily right away. I'm a regular writer, so I spend time secretly bouncing between two-year-old temper tantrums and a teenager's sullen angst when critiqued. And I still lose my equanimity with what can happen after I've again been told I don't include enough about my legs or wheelchair. The next paragraph of feedback is often something about how these omissions are signs that I'm not delving enough into my life, that I should "dig deeper," that I'm not writing in as honest a way as I could. I can deal with ignorant and disrespectful words, but now I'm being told I'm a dishonest writer. "Fuck you," I think.

Better description, digging deeper, writing honestly—all these, when not being used as an attack on a writer's self-awareness, are very good advice. So I glean from the emails, notes from the workshop, or scribbles on a page what's useful. An editor's examples of how I should delve more deeply can be terribly flawed and yet they lead me to finding other areas of silence that limit the piece. And later, maybe weeks or even years later, I appreciate the feedback about the ending, how it was too abrupt. And maybe right away, even as I am still reeling from the editor who makes sure I know the only reason they're considering my work is because they want more diversity, even then I know that the suggestion of changing the piece to third person is just what is needed.

I deserve the chance to become a better writer. I will not allow other people's prejudices or ignorance keep me from the knowledge of the writing craft they have to offer. And the few critiques that are wrong all the way through—

when I analyze, at length, all the ways they went sideways, it can provide insight. Even the straight-up, blithely unaware ableist comments are valuable. They clarify the cultural context that I'm writing within and help me parse out the high hum of bias that surrounds the more subtle incidents.

I've learned to ask of writers more accomplished than I am, each time it is possible, "What is the next thing I need to learn to make my writing better?" The late Maggie Estep told me, "Well, your dialogue sucks." She was right. I studied dialogue. Another writer told me (not in the context of my legs) that I stopped short emotionally. She said that I should write at least the next sentence. I could do that. It has made my writing better. An editor stabbed a pen at the next to last chapter and said, "Here's the end of your novel. Get rid of everything after." And I did. There is a great joy in getting criticism unmuddied by confusion about disability.

Have you noticed that I don't directly engage about egregious feedback? Other writers might respond to an editor, point out presumptions, and for better or worse, begin a dialogue. But I let those other people and their beliefs stew in their own prejudices and oppression. I don't care about them. I know, this is not the most activist stance, but picking battles gets you through a long life. And this lack of reaction isn't because I'm a coward or not an activist or just a weenie in general. (Maybe that last one is a little true.) It's because when I am unable to ignore someone coming at me with ableist crap or find a work-around that sidelines them or their power, I do fight back, I pick that battle.

For some people, this call to battle is what their work is all about. And what they write is magnificent. It changes our world. Entering into the fray can energize a writer. I've felt that—the heady joy of articulating anger, the sense of justice that comes from thoughtful analysis, the resplendent power of truth telling. And within all this, for me, something is always sacrificed. Every moment I'm forced to spend worrying or outraged instead of making my own life is a moment where words are left unwritten and exist only as fading shadows.

When I set out to write an essay or a story or a novel, I perhaps start with a word that resonates and the piercing of an emotion along with a fragment of dream or conversation. They combine into a shape that is both amorphous and powerful and has to be continuously built by folding it over and in on itself until form emerges. If in the middle of this momentum of construction, I'm diverted into a reaction to prove something or disprove something or make some sort of "up yours" statement or become obsessed about other people's obsessions about my legs, then the original story is gone. My energy is drained. I lose focus. What I end up writing instead has value, but the original story would have been my deepest delving, my most honest writing. Writing that, I believe, also might have had the power to change the world.

I don't know what would have happened had I been a young writer taking classes. My grades might have depended on responses to writing prompts that demanded my "most shameful moment," "biggest fear," or "worst family dinner." Long months of my childhood were spent in hospitals where my body was not my own, and I turn away from anything that either physically or emotionally mimics the hospital experience of unwanted poking and prodding. The young me wouldn't have known it was okay to lie and that no one was allowed to make me tell them anything. I'd learned to survive by being quiet and outwardly compliant. Perhaps I would have quit, since I was older before I added "and then go on and live my own life no matter what" to my silence. I'm proud of my boundaries. When I say, "I will tell you this but not that" or "I will tell you that but not in detail," it's liberating. And it is honest.

It's been a quarter of a century since my story about Barbara Stanwyck and the Shoney's waitress, the one where I gained the enthusiasm to continue and yet much was lost. The erased parts of that original story have always echoed within my personal essays, short stories, and novels. I'm a better writer than I was then. These echoes have become through lines that explore loneliness, power, desire, and the body's connection to the natural world. The forty-year-old writer I was then is contained within who I am now, and what was lost can be reclaimed.

BECOMING A DAUGHTER

"My mother and I share such a rich, spiritual time." At a friend of a friend's birthday potluck, this woman has overheard someone ask about my mother and is now exclaiming her own story of an aging parent. "We've reached a new plane of insight with each other. The beauty of her journey into old age inspires me." This woman smiles down at me. From my wheelchair height, I see teeth that haven't missed their last two cleaning appointments. She puts her hand down on my arm in a gesture meant to bond us. Next to her tan, my skin is the flat white found on the walls of rental apartments. And she's had the time to get a manicure.

A few years ago, my mother started to push the idea of me moving in with her. I lived a six-hour drive from her and had for a long time and that was on purpose. We were happy with our separate lives. We visited three times a year, which had always been enough interaction for the both of us. Yet now she was insisting on this new plan of hers each time we talked. I know now this is when she must have started losing her way and it scared her. But I didn't listen to her well enough. At first I laughed it off. Then I pushed back by explaining why I didn't want to upend my life. Finally, in a sort of desperation, I told her, "Mother this is never, ever going to happen."

Still, during each of our phone calls and my visits, as if

she'd never said it before, she told the story of bridge partners, the nurse taking her blood pressure, her neighbors, or
even a grocery store cashier, all of whom didn't understand,
given the "circumstances," why I didn't live with her. These
circumstances were never defined. My friends believed this
assumption of availability was a particular trial of the lesbian daughter, especially if single. I knew disability was in
the mix as well. I knew it would work for her to have me
around as a sort of servant while telling her bridge partners,
the nurse, the neighbors, and the cashier how she, even at
her age, was the one taking care of me. I was willing to help,
but I knew I needed my community of friends to make it
possible. So I sent her brochures for retirement communities near my home. She ignored them. It was a standoff.

One day she told me she became lost while driving in
her neighborhood of forty years. A police officer helped her
find her way home. It wasn't the first time, but I still didn't
know that. Soon after, she announced to her friends she
was moving closer to me. To take care of me, she told me
she told them. Since because of my "situation," I couldn't
handle things on my own anymore, she'd told them. She reported to me that her friends thought I was selfish to make
her move. She now lives in a retirement community seven
miles from me and is, and has every right to be, angry. She
had to leave the house my father built for her, her own community of friends, and everything she knows.

I'm at this birthday party because I told myself it was important for me to get out and socialize no matter how tired
I am. I told myself if I didn't, I might as well have moved
away and in with my mother. The woman who has reached
a new plane of insight removes her hand from my arm when
a second woman joins in on our conversation. "Oh, I know
what you mean. My mother, before she died, became my
best friend. I miss her every day." She puts her hand on the
first woman's shoulder. They have matching tears in their
eyes. I hate them.

Earlier in the day I took my mother to the grocery store. She becomes worried if I stray too far, so I followed behind her close, but not so close that my footrest hit her calves during her sudden stops and darts for cherries, raspberries, and blueberries. My mother and I have the same taste in fruit, but I can't afford berries. She handed me coupons for two-for-one Keebler cookies and one dollar off Campbell's cream of mushroom soup and asked me to find them. I veered away from her and reveled in the short time of freedom. I let my wheelchair go full speed down the aisles. While I searched for the sale items, I grabbed baking soda and on-sale grapes for myself. When I returned to her side, she pretended I wasn't there. The bus from my mother's retirement community had delivered a batch of her new neighbors, and she was socializing. A handsome octogenarian showed off his collapsible cart for carrying the groceries into his apartment. My mother flirted back. I hoped my mother would notice she could have been shopping without my help.

We checked out. I put my items on the counter. My mother said she'd pay for them. She always does, and this time, in advance, I'd decided to accept. The moment I did, she smiled that smile, and I knew I'd made a mistake. She said, "My, what a big portion of grapes. Won't they go bad before you can finish them?" She made a long-suffering face, and said to the cashier, "Isn't my daughter lucky to get all her food paid for?" When she told the bagger to only pack a few things into each bag, I said, "Remember, I told you it's easier for me to carry them for you if there are fewer bags." She said she needed a lot of bags. I said I was sure they would be glad to give her extra bags. The store staff was not looking at us anymore, but one of them stuffed a wad of bags in with our groceries.

As I opened the van door for my mother, I analyzed what had happened. Sure, she'd wanted to shame me, but also, she wanted to let the store people know it wasn't all one way, that she was helping me out in return for my help. I retaliated by making sure they knew her crippled-up daughter was going to do all the heavy lifting. Was I drawing a line against mistreatment, rewriting the childhood script where I was a burden, or being outright mean to the, these days, more and more emotional equivalent of a two-year-old? Was I the two-year-old?

Once the bags and my mother were loaded into the van, I made a point of thanking her for buying the baking soda and grapes for me. She said she was glad to, and she was just making a joke with the cashier.

After I unloaded and put away the groceries, my mother handed me the wooden saltshaker. "It won't work. You must have broken it during the packing." I reminded her I had fixed it a few days ago. "No," she said, "it hasn't worked since you made me move to this place." I rinsed out the clumped salt, dried it the best I could, and once again reminded her to let it air dry before refilling. I went to fetch her lunch from the cafeteria. When I returned, she was pouring salt into the shaker. While she was eating, I moved laundry from the washer to the dryer, refilled her medication dispenser, and fetched the mail. I made sure she wasn't at the door looking for me before I paused at the trash can to throw away all the scam emails seniors get. She was becoming more susceptible to them. When I returned, she said the portion of seafood lasagna I'd picked out wasn't very good, and I shouldn't have put her sweater in the dryer.

When I got home, I googled "power of attorney." I printed out the information and put it in the "Mother" file. I had an hour before the party. I could take a bath or rest. I transferred into bed and let the aches in my shoulders, elbows, back, knees, and ankles flare and then ease. When I woke to the alarm I'd set to avoid sleeping through until morning, I rubbed a washcloth into my armpits, put on something with a little cleavage, washed the grapes, arranged them in a nice bowl, and left for the birthday party.

And now I'm hating these women who are trying to be nice to me. This is a social event. I should wander away. Instead, I square my shoulders at the first woman. "So, you don't actually take care of your mother, do you?" My voice is combative. "Well, no. She has live-in help to do for her. But I call every Sunday. And I make sure to visit at least four times a year." The second woman pipes in. "And I was there with my mother every day the last week she was in the hospital. Even though she couldn't respond, it was a transformative experience."

If my mother were in a coma, my life would be transformed as well. How dare these women say a word? They know nothing. It's possible I've just snorted. But the mother-in-a-coma woman is oblivious. She looks down at me and says, "This time is a gift, isn't it?"

"Today, I thought of strangling my mother," I say. I make neck-wringing motions with my hands. "Sometimes it's a bag over her head."

This is untrue. But the truth—that I beat the steering wheel in the privacy of my closed-up van or sometimes during calls I grind the phone against a pillow until her voice is only a vibration under my palm—that truth wouldn't have obliterated the mother-love smugness off their faces. The two women look down on me with mirrored shock. I've accomplished the verbal equivalent of socking them in their jaws. I'm pleased. I'm also worried they'll be calling a senior abuse hotline.

"Hey, thanks for letting me blow off steam." I laugh, too high-pitched, and wave my hands around. "So, how long ago did your mother pass?" My face arranges itself into the appropriate expression. As I pretend to listen, I know I could have chosen to join in on this discussion of their spiritual journeys and transformations.

The day my mother called to say an apartment had become available in the retirement community near me and what did I think, my response was unhesitant and genuine.

My voice surprised me with its gentleness. "Move here," I said. "I'll help you." As much as I have disdain for the language these two women are using about their own, in my opinion, minimal caretaking, I can remember the peace, a seemliness, that settled in around me as my mother and I made plans for her move.

These days my mother and I are both angry and each for our own good reasons. But even when I'm screaming, "I hate you, you bitch!" at the dial tone of a hung-up phone, I've known this is the right thing for me to do. Not the "right thing" in some Mother Theresa, life-crushing duty way, but the right thing for me. It will be of benefit to me. My life will be better. Sometimes I try to add an ending. By caring for my mother I'll find love. (I think about the cute, butch nurse at her last doctor's appointment.) By caring for my mother I'll become a better writer. (Women have written bestselling books about their mothers.) That hasn't happened. The woman with the manicure is now talking about the grace and dignity conferred by caring for a beloved parent. I move my arm to the inside of the wheelchair's armrest, so her hand can't touch it again.

I want to be included. I want my experience to be part of the range of possibility of aging daughters. Women who tell me how they miss their mother every day, how they've never been happier since she moved in with them, how their mother is or was their best friend and how I'll feel the same way soon—they are not helpful. Also, I think they're lying. Intellectually, I know they might not be, but what they say, their emotions, are beyond my imagination.

Here's something to imagine. I don't like my mother and yet I have also had grace and dignity conferred on me by caring for her. Although it's an exhausted dignity with no pride or prestige, and the grace is awkward and shot through with resentment. And despite my scorn of the woman who said it, there have been gifts. It has been a gift to, for the first time, feel like someone's daughter. How would I have known I never had except by reflection? And it's a gift to have this puzzle piece slide into and fill what has been an absence of understanding.

I've become a daughter by joining the ancient, massive community of women who care for their mothers in their final years. I'm doing what daughters my age often do, and it doesn't matter that my mother and I are unbeloved to each other. For better and for worse, no matter their outrage or my judgment, I'm part of a community of daughters that includes both me and these two annoying women who are still standing uncomfortably close.

CRIP HUMOR

The patrol car barrels through the stop sign and pulls to a halt. I let my wheelchair slow, and the little dog matches my pace and then sits beside me when we come up alongside. The officer rolls down his window. Our heads are at the same level and close to each other. My neighbors around the corner, where this patrol car came from, have a cop for a son. He visits sometimes, and I figure this is him. He says, "I could give you a ticket." For many reasons, one of which is that I'm a white lady, I get to laugh. Not a snicker, but a belly guffaw, mouth wide open, that possibly sends spittle into his vehicle.

I also laugh because I think he's joking. One thousand one hundred fifty-two people (I did the math—an average of three times a month in the thirty-two years since I started using a wheelchair) have yelled at me that I'm going to get a ticket as I go by them in my wheelchair. I've been told and I've sometimes said myself that there's no harm meant. That, although tedious, these responses could be taken as a sort of encouragement or admiration.

Let me pause the story here to argue with my own self. There is harm meant. First of all, men (is it required that I say "not all men, not only men?") are yelling at a woman they don't know. Unless warning of an oncoming golf cart, a postthunderstorm-downed live wire, or a cottonmouth in the path (actual Florida incidents), the yelling itself is a hostile act. But what are they mad about? Perhaps they believe disabled people should never be fast, agile, graceful, competent, or seem as if they're having loads of fun. Me negotiating a sidewalk without hesitation with grocery bags hanging and swinging behind me, one hand on the joystick, and an arm wrapped around a bouquet with the flowers tickling my chin annoys them.

These men are tiresome. But I don't care because I am fast, agile, graceful, competent, and having a really good time. Especially when I have the little dog striding alongside me, ears back and tail bouncing. But this police officer in his patrol car must be friends with someone who uses a wheelchair and knows how funny he's being. He's to be lauded for taking the joke, that I think we are enjoying in common, to new heights what with him actually being able to give tickets. After all these long years, he's the first to elevate the cliché to a meta level, and I'm showing my appreciation with a long and loud laugh.

But the young officer turns face forward. His jaw bulges, and I am close enough to see the pounding beat of a blood vessel in his neck. Here's a man in a uniform who is angered by my disrespect. He turns his face back to mine and proclaims that he saw me run that stop sign with his own eyes. He says I'm in trouble. He keeps saying angry things and now the spittle is coming my way. I stop laughing, but I'm still smiling. Because this is even funnier than what I thought. And because my body believes in the protective cloak of disabled old lady whiteness.

And here's another pause in the story. I know people with disabilities make up a too large percentage of the too many people killed by police. I also know many of them are disabled black people and people with mental disabilities. I am neither of those. Still, I do move in a different way than what's considered regular. I've thought through how to respond if I'm pulled over in my car. My driver's license is in the side pocket of my wheelchair, which is behind my seat, which means I'd have to turn my seat around to get to it, which means I have to move my hand out of sight, dropping it down between the seats to toggle the control switches. And the seat's movements—swing sideways, up and down, and back—are sudden, fast, and can jerk. I've practiced how I would explain all these steps to an officer. And then how I would ask them for permission to perform each one.

But I don't tell anyone this. My preparations seem a sensible thing to do, but they are done dispassionately. It's as if I'm playacting the real danger of other people. The visceral truth for me in this moment and in other moments with police where I've actually been arrested (civil disobedience situations of a quarter century ago, drunk driving with the memory lost to a blackout) is that I have no fear lodged in my body that this interaction could go sideways in a violent way. I grew up in the military surrounded by drill sergeant types with puffed-out chests who barked orders in lieu of conversing. I learned early how to handle them, how to circumvent them. Except for the occasional spanking when I misjudged, I knew just how far to push against an over-inflated sense of authority. And the controlled and known pain of a spanking was experienced by me as mostly embarrassing and inculcated defiance rather than fear. Yet the statistics, the videos, the truth of people's lives say my body is wrong not to be wary.

The tirade ends with him yelling that I'm going to die. I have been recently diagnosed with breast cancer. And my body does remember the assault of childhood hospitalizations and has folded the memories into this recent surgery. He doesn't know about the cancer, but his threatening prediction still pisses me off with a sudden, harsh ferocity. I want to smack the side of his car and yell back that I am not going to die. So now we're both staring at each other with our eyes unblinking. The dog whines and pulls on the leash. She's right. It's time to deescalate. Maybe I also don't know something—maybe he has a loved one injured from a car running a stop sign.

I'm over, mostly, being the woman who is understanding and smiles that fake smile and says something conciliatory and self-deprecating, but right now someone has to do it. But I'm not going to address this young guy as "Sir," which is what my early training pushes me toward. All I can manage is to be quiet and not rant about the actual law and how a person who uses a wheelchair is legally considered a pedestrian and does he pull over joggers, who go much faster, as well or does he just think I'm incompetent because I'm disabled. I don't do that. Instead I blink, break eye contact, and look to the side, which is the body language that dogs use to avoid a fight. I can feel a muscle pull in my neck. He continues to consider what to do next. I don't care. If he gives me a ticket, fine. It'll be a hassle, but the judge might dress him down in front of everyone in court. That would be fun. If he doesn't give me a ticket, the little dog and I will go on with our stroll. Either way, I have a story to tell. The little dog snorts her annoyance at us. He drives off.

I do tell this story, and I tell it in a simplified-almost-to-the-point-of-inaccuracy way. After a quick acknowledgment of the complexities, I make it entertainment. Those of us who use wheelchairs and those who hang out with us are the ones who squeal in recognition and laugh until the perhaps the few stomach muscles we have left ache or we pee a little in our pants. Other people can't figure out where the funny is because they think the officer was in the right and then they lecture me about safety. The story, told this way, has become a study of cultural differences in humor perception. And an example of there being a disability culture.

The story, as I tell it at dinner parties, has value. And it is incomplete in ways I understand and in ways—no matter how much outrage, mourning, and despair I feel with each recounting of free-range police violence—I'll never understand. Besides its own experience, how can a body learn?

Can it learn innate wariness through the witness of other people's experience? Can the rationality of lists and statistics teach it more than sympathetic concern?

What my body knows is to be oppositional. Sometimes that meant and sometimes still means saying "Yes, sir" and then sneaking. Sometimes it means showing up on the street to put itself in the way. My aging body strives to be uncooperative, fractious, and cranky. So I sometimes look both ways for the patrol car at that quiet neighborhood four-way stop two doors down from my house. Which means I do slow down, as the police officer would have wished. But I'm ready. If he's there, lurking, I'm toggling the wheelchair speed to high and yelling "Go, go, go!" to the little dog. All he'll see is eighteen pounds of terrier lunging against her leash and the blur of an old woman with her gray hair streaming. Come on, give us a chase.

SPANISH LESSONS

The small table in my small apartment is crowded with a dictionary, cups of tea, and a worksheet of verb conjugations. Our elbows find the last clear space as Maria and I hunch over the book spread between us. I keep my arm fixed in place as her elbow shifts and the hair of our forearms mingle. Maria reaches to turn the page and cool air moves in along my skin.

Maria is helping me translate another poem. This one is by a lesbian from Argentina, and I can already tell that it's a sad tale. I arch my spine and hold it through the ache. I put my palms down to push against the seat of the wheelchair and shift my weight from hip to hip. I've become accustomed to the way soreness travels under my skin. Today it centers in my back and wings along the lower ribs.

Maria reads the next stanza with the careful enunciation she uses for my benefit. I stare at the grease splatter on the wall over the stove. When had that happened? What else in the apartment is layered in a grime I haven't noticed? Maria used the bathroom earlier. Had it been disgusting? I look at her profile. She doesn't look disgusted. I push my chair back from the table and lift one ankle over a knee. Maria's voice continues. I shut my eyes and let the silkened consonants roll by. I can't tell if things are happening, have happened, or will happen, but I recognize nouns: a purple sky, a street, music from far away, the one who cries, and the dead. When I open my eyes again, the wall clock comes into focus.

It's been an hour. In all that time, my only worry has been about a failure in housekeeping. And I sat with my back to the door. A strange mix of pride but mostly alarm straightens my posture. The alarm makes me push my foot off my knee and let it drop back to the footrest. I twist to look over my shoulder. The door is ajar; Maria must have left it open when she came in. I have not been vigilant. I didn't make sure. And I'm not wearing shoes. I need my shoes. I release the brakes and swing over to the kitchen chair where I keep them. I shove them on. Where are my car keys? I feel down into the bag strapped under the seat and relax a little when my fingertips touch the keys. Maria clears her throat. I don't know how to explain. I don't look at her, but I come back to the table, bend my head over the poem, and stab a fingernail at the page to underline a phrase.

"This line, las gotas de sangre. What are las gotas?"

Drops of blood fan along the neck of a bereaved woman. The lesson continues. Maria's voice lifts the stanzas into the air between us, but the words blur into rhythms of slurred vowels and I lose hold on my ability to understand. Some of the words are familiar. I remember having known what they mean. I do know that the open door is an itch at the back of my neck, and I ache with the need to go lock it. I should have just done that when I first noticed and then it would have been taken care of, but being afraid just pisses me off so I hadn't and now I can't concentrate. Maria stops reciting and is watching again.

"Let's go somewhere." I always feel better out of the apartment. I'm stacking books and gathering papers before Maria even answers.

"Está bien. The park?"

We had met at a Thanksgiving potluck at Opal's, and Maria, Opal's new roommate, was reading women's palms. I'd lingered at the edge of the room. Women set food on the dining room table and settled into the couch, easy chairs, and folding chairs brought in for the occasion. On the porch, the smokers' conversations wafted in. Old friends kissed hello and complimented new clothes and new jobs and introduced new girlfriends around. I'd regretted I hadn't at least gotten a haircut. I watched how Maria cupped women's elbows in her hand as she told their fortune. I couldn't hear what was said, but noticed the way women leaned toward Maria. Some perched their bodies over one hip, others dropped their shoulders away from their ears. Arms relaxed to hang loose or fingers touched at their own neck and hair. Maria was egalitarian. She didn't skip anyone as she made her way among us. There was nothing predatory in her manner. Perhaps this was her way of introducing herself to everyone. I was glad the "Let's eat!" sounded from the kitchen before it was my turn.

It was after the meal but before the pies, and I was at the sink taking my turn washing dishes. The work soothed me, and I kept at it until the last glass possible was balanced on top of the stack in the drainer. When I turned to the side and shook my hands in the air to dry, water splattered over Maria's chest. Maria tried to reach past me to leave her own dish in the sink as I tried to leave the kitchen. We exchanged a chorus of "So sorry" and "Perdón" until I was finally past her. She followed me through the door. She touched my shoulder.

"I will tell your fortune?"

I held out an arm. It must have been the soothing properties of turkey and buttered mashed potatoes that made it possible. Maria cradled my hand the way she had the others and pulled open my fingers. She touched into the still damp palm and traced a crease. Even through the haze of overeating, my skin responded. It was subtle. A small motion of electrons. But I twitched in surprise, and my arm pulled itself back close to my body. Maria clasped her now empty hands together at her chest and tilted them toward me.

"Do you know Spanish?"

I shook my head.

"Your wisdom line says this year you will learn. May I teach you?"

At the park, a boardwalk winds through a Florida hammock of hardwoods and palms. In the winter dryness, oak leaves crack underneath. Maria kicks sweetgum pods down the trail. Ancient tree limbs curve close to the ground and up again. Maria sits on one and swings her feet.

I ask, "Como si dice 'oak"?"

"Roble," she answers.

I point at the tall unfurling of a cinnamon fern.

"Los helechos," she says.

I had loved living in Florida. And today, in January, outside, comfortable with just a vest, I do again. I ask Maria about the weather in Venezuela.

"Hace calor. Never so cold as here." She shivers, hops to the ground, and puts her hand on my shoulder as we continue along the path. I expect the pressure to hurt, but it doesn't. Still, I stop in place and let Maria pull ahead. She turns and waits. I almost explain, but instead I find a woodpecker to point at.

"El pájaro carpintero," she answers.

As we continue down the path together, I do speak.

"Tell me more about Venezuela."

Maria gestures with a large sweep of her arms. They fling open to describe the immensity of La Gran Sabana, high plains where anacondas live in the grasses. Her forearms curve around each other in an imitation of slithering. Then Maria rises until she's on tiptoe with both arms stretched over her head. Her fingertips beat against the sky. Tepuyes—mesas, unexplored and massive—rising out of the earth so high they have their own weather.

"Did you live there?"

"Oh, no. We live in cities with the trash and the violence." Maria's arms hug around her own body. "But los llanos, the plains, they are our corazón salvaje, how do you say it, the wildness that lives in our hearts. Y tú? Where is your heart home?"

"Here in Florida, I guess." But I don't think I have a heart home.

We continue down the trail close together and in silence. At the bridge, we lean on the railing and look along the creek bed. It won't have water until the summer rains, but the smell of dampness and rich muck promises something.

I imagine climbing a tepuye using ropes, a pulley, and a harness. It would take many days, and sometimes I would pause to rest and lean backward over the world so far below. Sometimes I would almost fall. I imagine the moment of grabbing for the next outcrop, as I had been doing again and again, but touching nothing because I will have reached the top. I will roll over the edge and lie face up on the floor of a forest. The blooms of unknown orchids will hang over my belly, and at my feet ferns, helechos, will grow into the sky. Pools of water will overflow the edges in long waterfalls. I'll become a heretofore unknown species of bird, rainbow feathered, riding the water mist back to the savannah, where I'll skim low over grasses that shake in an endless wind. The shadow of my wings will cause a stirring among the animals that live hidden on the earth.

"How long are those anacondas, Maria?"

"Seven meters, más o menos."

I calculate meters to feet, remember the word for "liar," and slap at Maria's shoulder.

"Mentirosa."

"Es la verdad." Maria steps in front me and walks backward. She trips over roots as she points down to trace along the ground.

"All the way to here. Once, in a biológica park, I saw one. Maravillosa."

I look down the path, down the long stretch of snake between us. I have no idea if Maria is making it up, maybe having a little fun with the gringa. It doesn't matter. I've yet to find any malice in this woman. I grab my wheels and swerve to match the curves of our imaginary snake. I fake being grabbed and jerk away to release the coil wrapped around an axle. Freed, I race past Maria. She follows and claps and leaps around me. We rush down the trail together and invent dangers to survive.

"Right in front of us, an alligator." I shout it at a root across our path. Maria leaps, and I hop the casters over its growling, gaping mouth.

"Watch out, las tarántulas," and we duck under a golden orb weaver's glistening web.

I stop to catch my breath and am suddenly certain that I will sleep that night for the entire night, that I will wake into a new day instead of the lost, late hours of a yesterday. A dog barks in the distance. I windmill my arms before I drop them, elbows up, on the wheels.

"Los lobos have our scent. Run."

We squeal all the way back to the parking lot.

Running didn't help. It just turned you into prey. I remember the exact moment I learned this. It had been weeks since she'd finally moved out. I didn't think she knew about my Wednesday night bookbinding class. But I saw the familiar car advance, idle, and then creep forward as it hunted through the parking lot of the elementary school where the class was held. I'd been found. I looked for somewhere to hide. There was a pillar perhaps wide enough. I secured the bag of supplies and the half-finished journal with its Japanese stab binding on one of the push handles. I moved to the shadowed side of the pillar. My hands fisted into the sides of my thighs. A classmate startled when he came upon me. He asked if I needed help with anything.

"Just have to retie a shoe. I'll be right in." I faked leaning over.

He left. I timed him as he crossed the courtyard to the classroom. Twenty-eight seconds. I could do it faster. And I had to follow him, since he'd seen me. If I didn't show up, they'd be concerned, maybe even call the police. It would be embarrassing to have to explain. I moved into the open. It was dusk. Across the courtyard, the fluorescent lights in the classroom window flickered on. Nothing had ever happened in front of other people. I set out toward the lights.

Ten seconds later, I heard my name called. The voice reached for me. It was triumphant. I thought I could smell almond shampoo. I hated that smell. I stopped and turned. The next choice was mine. Would I try to rush away? Or would I stay put and hiss out angry words? This was the moment when I understood. With either choice, I was prey that had been brought down. Some ancient knowledge said to disappear, go inert, become erased. My eyes glazed over, my muscles went slack, and my heartbeat slowed. I hadn't known I could do this. I nodded as if to a stranger and not a wisp of emotion escaped me. It confused her. I turned before she saw my small smile and pushed in a steady way to the classroom door. No one followed me. No one yelled at me. No one grabbed the back handles of my wheelchair to hold me in place.

Once at the worktable, I waited for some sense of triumph. I'd succeeded. But it turned out there wasn't any winning. Once I emptied myself of emotion, everything was gone. I cut leather cords and assembled folios, but the pleasure of creating had disappeared. At the end of the two hours, I made appropriate admiring comments about my classmates' work. I listened as the others debated the pros and cons of deckle edges and shared their sources for cover papers. I waited to leave with a group. I never went back.

It had been another of our Spanish lesson days, and now I'm hanging on to the open refrigerator door. I'm hungry, but nothing seems worth cooking. The pork chops have turned gray under their plastic wrap. The thought of chopping vegetables makes me think of all the vegetables I've ever chopped. No matter what I decide to eat, I'll have dirty pots to clean and more food to shop for and put away, and after that, I'll end up leaning on the fridge door staring again. And I'll be doing this for the rest of my life. And today my neck hurts. I reach for the cottage cheese and a can of pineapple. Condiments rattle when I shut the door.

The lesson had been at Maria's. I'd pulled my car into the driveway and seen quilts spread over the yard. It was a wood house with no insulation, and on a February day it was warmer to sit outside in the sun. Maria, Opal, and Opal's date from the night before wore layers of sweaters and scarves and looked pastoral as they lounged over the patchwork of colors. Except they were shouting at each other. Maria's voice was almost shrill. I kept the car in gear until I heard laughter winding through the commotion. By the time I got out, Maria was flushed and alternating her languages as she yelled "Cállate!" and then "Shut up!" Opal and her date argued back and forth. "Butch." "Are you kidding, she's way femme." Opal got up on her knees and outlined Maria's body with wiggling fingertips. "Excuse me, but all this—smokin' hot butch." Opal waved me over.

"Great, you're here just in time to settle things."

I moved close enough to be sure no one was really angry. Opal and the date kept teasing Maria. She wrapped a shawl around her jeans and hitched her hips in a merengue rhythm while Opal tried to tuck a dollar bill into her waistband. I envied their ease with each other and tried to think of something clever to say. I decided it was too risky. Moods could change in an instant. Maria minced closer and held out her hand palm up. I kept mine out of reach and a sadness poured over me. I didn't want to be this person anymore. I wanted something else.

Maria dropped the shawl and said something in Spanish that none of us understood. She went into the house. She came back out with the textbook and motioned for me to follow her to a far corner of the quilts. I slid down out of my chair as she opened the book between us and said "Comienza" in a quiet voice.

The lesson, this one about the names of appliances, had been yet another story with a wife in the kitchen. Maria changed it around. In her version the woman turned off the oven, told her husband to do his own cooking, took her washing machine and dryer, and moved in with the lovely Rosita, where they lived in a pretty house with its own microwave and a built-in dishwasher. I learned how to say "Happily ever after" in Spanish. Later we sat cross-legged in front of each other and ate strawberries and cream. I sucked the last of the cream off the spoon and asked Maria to tell me another story. She talked of being fourteen and visiting the Italian side of her family and meeting una prima, an older distant cousin, and falling in love for the first time.

When the tale ended, Maria had tilted her chin at me and said "Y tú?" I pretended not to understand. I said I had to leave. I didn't have to pretend I was stiff from sitting on the ground. Once I'd lifted back up into the chair, I held the side of my neck and stretched it from side to side. Today, that's where the soreness had settled. Maria stood up with me, behind me, and massaged where neck met shoulder. Panic slid around inside me, but I didn't pull away. When Opal shouted from the house that Maria had a phone call, I pulled the collar of my sweater closed and skittered toward the car. I said goodbye without turning around. The imprint of being touched lingered as I backed the car into the street. At home, I contorted in front of the mirror to look at my neck. It always seemed as if there should be bruises. My skin was unmottled and smooth.

And now I sit in front of the television with a bowl propped on my breasts and scoop canned pineapple into my mouth while watching an old *Star Trek* episode. Deanna Troy is doing her empathic Betazoid counseling thing. I sob into the cottage cheese. Later, the phone rings but I don't answer it. Much later, I turn off the television, drop the bowl in the sink, and check the chain on the door. I should scrub the grease behind the stove. I straighten the dish towel. I push the toaster oven flat against the wall and linger in the kitchen with one hand resting on the counter. The clock ticks. A car alarm goes off, not close, but close enough that I jerk.

At the end of winter, I had a dream. In it I was a healer, certain of my place in the universe. I was a woman of infinite kindness, a kindness without undue sentiment, a kindness that understands how the world is, what is necessary. I took great care making the poisoned tea. Steam filled the room with complex aromas. I made sure of the temperature. It was hot but wouldn't scald. I placed the brew into the waiting palms and made sure they had a good grip on the mug. I placed my own hands around them and touched the pulse in each wrist. Together we raised the mug. I watched the liquid slide over the tongue. I saw the throat tighten and release. Together, we lowered the mug. My fingertips felt the quickened rise of the blood. The eyes in front of me widened, and I reassured with a smile of gentleness and peace. The eyes closed. The beat under my fingers diminished. Death was close. Death was generous. Death was necessary.

I woke up knowing it was done. I took all my art and photographs down and liked the blankness of the walls. I cleaned the kitchen cabinets. I sorted and refolded all the clothes in my chest of drawers. I thought about the dream.

Beyond the obvious, I was unsure of who or what had died. Of what came after death. I rehung all the pictures but in a new configuration. At a yard sale I found a blanket with a pattern of yellow and brown stripes and used it to brighten the back of the couch.

It's April and we're sprawled over a yellow blanket spread on the slope of a lake. I sit with my arms around my knees, and flocks of gulls and an occasional osprey fly by. Maria lies on her back with a jacket bunched under her head.

"El lago," she instructs.

"Los pajaros blancos," I reply.

It's not much of a lesson. The afternoon heats up, and we take off more clothes and pile them around the periphery of the blanket along with a cooler, dictionary, and textbook. We're almost down to the last layers possible at a state park. I've even slipped off my pants and am pretending my shirt is a very short dress. Maria stands, takes off her flannel shirt, and rolls the sleeves of her T-shirt over her shoulders. I take off my socks and stretch my legs out straight. Today the pain is in my knees. I press my hands onto them and the heat of my palms soaks into my skin and wraps around the hurt. Sunlight reflects off my shins. A breeze warms my toes.

Maria drops, legs crossed, beside me. She has a sandwich in each hand and holds one out. Turkey and guacamole, she announces. She pulls a bag of chips from under her arm, puts it between us, and places a napkin on each of our laps. The feather weight of the paper tickles my thigh. I'm about to say that for the next lesson, I'll be the one to bring lunch, but just in time I stop myself and accept her kindness. Today, in the spring sun, in front of the lake, I want to try not to say no, not to refuse, not to ignore. I bite into the sandwich. The creamy green garlicked taste mixes with the salt of the deli meat. I reach into the chip bag, and Maria holds it steady.

We watch the lake while we chew. An alligator rises above the surface. Maria tells another story. When she first arrived, people said not to swim in this lake. Because of alligators, they said. She had thought they were kidding and making fun of her for being a foreigner and ignorant. "Like anacondas," I say. "Yes, just like that. A danger for real," she says. The alligator drops lower. Eyes and the tip of a snout linger and then there's only a flat place on the surface of the water. Maria lies down with a sigh and puts an arm over her face to block the sun.

"Ahora, la instrucción." She uses her teacher voice. I turn onto my stomach and look at the open textbook.

"Clauses associated with the subjunctive mood." I stop reading and pull my jacket over, fold it, place it on top of the book, and pillow my head into the fleece.

"Es mejor que we take a nap, don't you think?"

Maria lifts her arm and opens her eyes. They are inches from mine. She has green eyes.

"Perezosa." Maria's forearm goes back down over her face.

I curl onto my side. I do feel lazy—lazy in a grand, almost forgotten way. When I reach around to make sure my bottom is covered, I feel Maria's hip less than an inch away. Outside, under the sky, with no doors and no locks, I rest.

I have no idea what time it is. I've been asleep, I know that. The wind from the lake finds its way under my improvised dress before it goes on to rattle through the palmetto fronds behind me. I notice that I'm happy. One knee still hurts, but that's from a rock under the blanket. I shift away from it. I open my eyes. The afternoon brilliance has changed to the bronzed colors that happen only briefly and only when the light angles low.

An unknown sound makes me sit and look over the lake. It's the rush of air from the downbeat of wings. A bald eagle skims the top of the water, and with a precise surge of power, its talons dip under the surface. The bird's body keeps moving forward while its legs pull back. The claws, with a fish speared in one of them, clear the surface. The eagle pauses midair and adapts to the new weight before it curves into the sky.

I feel an inquiring palm in the small of my back and point to the eagle on a distant pine tree. Maria's hand drifts up my spine. I think about birds and how strong their shoulders must be to hold wings, to dive, to survive. I lean my head close to Maria's shoulder. Before we put all our layers of clothing back on, as the sun touches the treetops across the lake, I tell a story. Maria listens as the afternoon wind falls silent and all the colors fade to gray.

PREPARING FOR THE FALL

The lid must have been loose, because when I lift the bottle out of the refrigerator it falls and a spray of pills scatters over the kitchen floor. The dog, alert to the sound of a possible snack, charges out of the bedroom. I tell her to go to her crate. Which she does. Which is good, since even one of these pills would make her sick.

I lean over my wheelchair and pick up the circle of pills I can reach and then sit back up, tap on the joystick to move the wheelchair a few inches, push my butt to the back of the seat for balance, and, as I stretch my arm over my head and down, lean over again to retrieve the next batch of pills now in reach. One of them rolls from under my fingertips, and I extend just that little extra, that little bit too far. I've fallen out of my wheelchair before. In the second between knowing no recovery is possible and hitting the ground, it works best to imagine myself having already fallen and moving on to a solution.

I had polio as a baby, and my first braces and crutches meant I no longer had to be carried everywhere. It must have been a wondrous sense of freedom for a two- or maybe three-year-old. From early on, my palms could interpret the small movements transmitted up the wooden and then aluminum shafts as the rubber crutch tips stuttered against, slipped on, or stuck into snow, mud, thick grasses, oily pavement, or the shifting of gravel.

Still, I would fall. I'd bounce easily onto the ground the way kids can and my crutches would flail into the air like ski poles. Almost as quickly as I'd fallen, I'd have my butt up in the air with my legs locked straight by my braces. My dress would flip over my head. I'd make sure my crutches were wedged tight in front of me and then I'd climb them, hand over hand, to standing. By the time I was five I knew this was immodest, so I'd pull the knee-release levers and kneel. Elbows akimbo, crutches angled out from my body, I'd lift up between them in a display of joyful strength. Each time I was knocked down—by a patch of black ice, by a tangle of feet and elbows in a crowd, by the kids and later a fellow university student who grabbed a crutch away from me to see what would happen—I'd find my pride again in my skills and the power of my arms.

Sprawled on the kitchen floor, I begin by assessing injuries. I hold my shin where it has scraped against a footrest and test out the hip I've fallen on. Nothing is broken or bleeding. I hurt but not in a scary way. I sit up, pull my legs together, and think about how I'm going to get back into the chair. I'm not sure, so I use the time to gather the rest of the pills. From this new angle I can determine that none have rolled under the door of the refrigerator or into the crack between the stove and the counter that I can see is in need of cleaning. The dog leaves her crate to come sniff at me, curious about the way I've joined her on the floor. I should send her back to reinforce her waiting until I say it's okay, but instead I scratch her ears for my own comfort, while I think more about how to get up.

Falling out of my wheelchair hasn't been common over the years, but it happens. When I used a manual wheelchair, it was low enough and I was still strong enough to get on my knees facing the chair, grab the armrests, and use leverage, the heft of my breasts, and my arm strength to raise my body into the seat. With a dramatic lift and twist, I'd plop face front smug and flush with accomplishment. But that was twenty years ago. The short while I used a scooter taught me about being narrow and top-heavy like a sailboat. By "taught" I mean a drop along the edge of a hiking trail would put me in a slow-motion sideways tilt that allowed enough time to grip the handle with one hand and straight-arm out to a tree trunk or all the way to the ground to stop the fall. My position mimicked that of a sailor leaning horizontal over the water, into the wind, to keep their boat from swamping. If I was with a companion, they could easily push me upright. If I was alone, I could reach the throttle with my thumb and inch the scooter forward while hopping my other hand along the ground until I reached a rock or tree trunk to bounce upright from.

The bathroom seems a good first choice. Maybe I can get up onto the toilet seat and from there into the wheelchair. Plus, I really have to pee. I slide backward a half foot, strain forward until a finger can reach the joystick, and carefully move the four-hundred-pound wheelchair up to but not over my legs. But then I remember what I've forgotten. These days, I'm not alone. I leave the wheelchair and scoot on my rear end over the heart pine floors to retrieve the cell phone charging at my bedside. My wife, Pam, is working in the cottage behind the house. I don't call her. The habit of figuring things out for myself is not something I'm willing to give up. This is sometimes an issue between us. I scoot back to the wheelchair, sliding the phone along with me, and resume the six-inches-at-a-time trip to the bathroom.

The moment I lift my butt over the threshold to the bathroom, I know this is a bad plan. From my position on the floor, the toilet seat is obviously too high. The daybed in the writing studio is lower. I repeat the slow trek to the front of the house.

It took me a while to get used to the weight and velocity of a power chair. Hazards included the moles who excavate tunnels just under the surface of a yard. My front wheels would collapse the tunnel, sink, and throw the wheelchair to an abrupt stop. I'd sometimes fly out onto the ground. I learned, after spraining an ankle, to inspect agility fields before doing an obstacle course with my dog. I became skilled at noticing the churned-up lines of sand that signal the danger. Which helped with yard work, which, in Florida, is mostly cutting back and pulling up. The first time I had a wheelchair that included tilt and recline options, which means it's much heavier and more likely to become mired, I ended up on the ground. I knew I couldn't muscle my way back up anymore. But the immediate danger was being in sight of the road in front of my house. I scooted behind the wheelchair to hide. A car will screech to a stop, the driver will rush out, ignore everything I say, and wrench my shoulders to pull hard on my arms as if that's all I need to be able to stand. So I hid except to fish out my cell phone from the pack hanging on the armrest.

In the timeline of my mobility aids, the cell phone appeared post braces and crutches, post manual wheelchair, post scooter, post the first two power chairs. I had loads of falls, dead batteries, and breakdowns pre–cell phone that were always figured out. Obviously, I at no time died lost on an isolated trail after my wheelchair was stuck in the mud or was stranded forever when a tire blew. But I've been glad of having more technology to substitute for the lessening of physical ability. So still hiding from the danger of a rescue-happy public, I called a friend to come help me. She could be there in forty-five minutes. I spent the time pulling up Boston ferns and invasive ardisia plants. Later, I considered how, if I could fit enough of my rear end on a footrest and if the footrest would support my weight, I could have used the tilt and recline to lift me level to the seat. Later I practiced this strategy and it was successful but came close to snapping the footrest. In the future, it wouldn't be my first choice.

With each new chair, I've had to recalibrate how far forward, down, and sideways I can safely reach by making an internal, mostly intuitive, computation that considers the seat height, my current trunk strength, and the best point of fulcrum where the end of the armrest digs in and supports my ribs when I lean. And I have to be barefoot or have shoes on with soles that stick hard to the footrests. My always-changing current strength is where I have most often misjudged.

By the time I make it to the writing room, I'm cold, which weakens my muscles. I'd planned to pop out of bed, take some pain meds, go pee, and get back in bed. So I am naked. And smeared with dust and debris. From my angle on the floor, the writing bed seems possible. I pull a pillow down to put under my knees and use the stability of the wheelchair footrests to pull up. My knees shake right away, but I'm able to throw my torso onto the mattress before they collapse. My fingertips graze but won't wrap around the far railing of the daybed, the coverlet is too loose to provide any purchase, and there's nothing else to grip and pull myself the rest of the way. I hang suspended. This is annoying. But what I need now is someone to come position one knee up, and I'd be able to roll myself onto the mattress. I call Pam. At least I'll be offering up quite the view.

The next day my shin develops the purple black of a deep bruise, which becomes a dramatic storytelling aid when I make my friends laugh about me mopping the floor with my butt. The other leg twisted over itself on the way down, and the pain from ankle to knee to hip to back isn't funny and isn't something I talk about.

Falling is the great divide for the aging. It doesn't matter that I've been falling for over sixty years. A single fall with no injury is no longer just an accident, a careless mistake, or a regular part of a lived life. Instead, my ability to make my own decisions, any decisions, becomes suspect. So I stick with the funny naked story and keep my worries that it could have been a broken leg, or worse an arm, to myself. The bruise fades and the leg pain diminishes.

I used to lift myself out of a pool. I'd place my hands on the edge, level to where my head bobbed, and rise, emerging like Venus, a Venus with massive shoulders that tapered down to short twisted legs and tiny feet. I'm sixty-six now and that strength is gone. I'm not as graceful in movement as I used to be when I could swing a door open, twist the wheelchair into position, and slide past the door before it closed. These days I'm more likely to scrape my knuckles.

Instead of being a funny naked story, the next fall could be the one where they say "—and it went downhill from there." But I'm coming into old age with already honed adaptive techniques. So before I reach down to pick up the dog's water bowl or retrieve the lapful of mail that slid off my knees, I find something sturdy to brace on—a doorjamb, a table edge, the nonpatronizing help of a friend. I have a community of mutual support. Some of us have been friends since coming together in the lesbian-feminist surge of the 1980s, so they are aging alongside me. We watch out for each other. The dog has decided she's old now as well and doesn't have to do much of what I ask, which I, in theory, support. But she still fishes out pens that have rolled under the bed and tosses them onto my lap.

Nevertheless, the next fall could be the one where my loved ones, the medical establishment, or perhaps even I succumb to "I've fallen and can't get up" fearmongering for profit. It will be decided the fall wasn't an accident or dumb mistake on my part. I will no longer have agency, for good or bad, over my own body, and the whispers of "Something must be done" will begin. Of course, there are increased consequences to falling as we age. But if there were less of a stigma about using canes, walkers, wheelchairs, or asking to take a friend's arm, falls could be more often prevented. Because how does a button around your neck prevent a fall? More to the point, what imagined social stigma am I still avoiding? What adjustments should I accept?

So I'm careful and I worry. A slip of my wrist transferring from wheelchair to bed, a moment of inattention that leads to a wrenched shoulder, or one of those regular things old people get like a heart attack or bad lungs scares me. The new skills and help I'd have to ask for, if, say, I have surgery on my shoulder and can't transfer on my own while it heals, seem overwhelming. And this is despite knowing people who live successful, interesting, complicated lives without having ever been able to transfer on their own. These are people who negotiate getting help in a practical and skilled way that I can't yet imagine.

I'm careful. Still, there can be a sleepy morning where a loose cap on a pill bottle and a minor misjudgment ends with me on the floor. That ended up a relatively small problem, and those are best approached with a sense of humor. But I know I'll fall again. This is a moment in-between. This is when I prepare for that fall.

HOW TO RELEASE A REJECTED NOVEL

First, grieve. Have a little cry as you move the novel's folder out of your computer's sidebar. We used to call this stashing it in a bottom drawer. Have an angry cry as you scroll down the submission chart with all those rejections coded in red font. The color dominates. Despite telling yourself not to, you reread the scattered blue-coded notes that recall the heart-squeezing moments of requests for more. You remember hope. Then move the chart into the "Retired Submissions" folder. Whine about how the last five years of work having been for nothing. Which even as you whimper, you know isn't true. Months, perhaps years later you reread the novel and the truth is there are unfixable flaws. In a weird way it makes you feel better.

Second. Move a new file into the computer's sidebar. It doesn't matter if it's empty. If you're finally regaining some of your writer hubris, label it "Current Novel in Progress." Open a new document and try to make an outline of this figment of a novel because you want to be someone who makes outlines this time around. You aren't. Still, you write a swirl of quick scenes and emotionally fraught moments. You save it into the new file. It is no longer empty.

———————

Third. And this is essential. Have a party. A "book-release" party. Invite everyone you know. Tell them they have to bring a gift. You admire the altruistic who tell us that no gift is required or ask us to donate to this or that charity. They are wonderful people. You are not one of them. Some of us have discretionary income and some of us do not, so you define "gift" as including the nonmaterial.

The party. It is celebratory. You've made bookmarks for everyone with quotes from the novel on one side and lovely photos on the other. Some of the guests are other writers, and they've composed poems for the occasion. Others are avid readers and perform their favorite passages. Some bring you gift cards to Office Depot, and you exclaim that now you have more money for ink cartridges. (You are one of the ones with minimal discretionary income.) A friend who has no clue about the publishing world or why you are even having this party appears in the doorway staggering under the weight of a box. She has to squat to brace it on her knees and readjust her grip before she can step into the house. The box is full of paper. Ten reams. That's fifty pounds, five thousand sheets. Oh, the possibilities. And now the book is released.

But this is not the end of the story. I did write a second novel that was published. And I did pull that first novel out of its metaphorical bottom drawer. Its fatal flaw was the one common to many first novels, which was being autobiographical but not in the good way. I used that. I disassembled the parts. Some became the ideas for short stories, and many segments became what they really were—personal essays. I edited out the made-up parts and put in more of my own self. And some of those essays did get published. And I liked having more blue text on my submission chart, so I wrote more essays. And more were published. Eventually, I created a new file folder named "Possible Memoir," plopped it into the sidebar, and set about assembling the writings. I created a new submission chart that also filled with rejection red but ended, after five years of trying, with a final jubilant burst of blue. This book-release party was also fabulous and celebratory but with more tenderness. This sweetness came from those of us who remembered that first party. A friend would hand me a book to sign. I'd open it up to the title page and find one of the bookmarks, faded and frayed, from twenty years ago.

THE LAST PARTY

In 1992 I and a bunch of disability rights activists were arrested for protesting outside the annual convention of the nursing home industry. Here was an organization that lobbied their way into control of billions dollars of public monies meant for our care. It didn't seem right that they were drinking margaritas poolside while so many of us were trapped in nursing homes. Often this was for no other reason than that the money could not be paid directly to us for home care but only to nursing homes. So there I was in Orlando storming the gates of a luxury hotel.

Seventeen years later, I've been touring nursing homes without telling my mother what I'm doing. I visited five of them this week. Beckie, a friend who looks very able-bodied, goes with me to some of them. The first one is a warehouse plain and simple. The occupants are mostly African American. The management has obviously packed two beds into what used to be an already tiny single room, which means I, in my wheelchair, would only be able to wave at my mother from the hall. And no matter how clearly I state my reason for being there, how well I have dressed in preparation (because I knew this would happen), how official I've made myself look with a file folder and pen at the ready, they think Beckie is there to admit me. The next one is a warehouse as well, but with better light. The racial makeup is mixed. I pass a resident in the hall. His wheelchair is similar to mine. He's younger than I am. Why is he here? I leave, frightened for myself again. The third is less of a warehouse. The staff and residents are out roaming the halls and gardens, they call to each other by name, everyone is loud and cheerful. And yes, the residents are mostly white. Later, when I investigate online, all these places fail their inspections in many categories. There is no nursing home in Gainesville rated above a three out of five. All of them have waiting lists. I've put my mother on them.

I tell the hospice social worker that I've done this. I tell her which one I like the best, but it has a long waiting list. She asks if I told them that my mother would be private pay. No, I say. The hospice nurse has come up to stand with us. They look at each other. "Sandra," the social worker says, "I'll go speak to them and let them know the situation." I come to understand that there are lists and then there are lists. The social worker gets her serious look and continues, "But first I need to know if you are prepared to go forward. It can happen quickly."

I can't answer. My brain twists through a loop of questions. Is it the correct perspective that my mother is in a final sort of decline and that any single good moment doesn't change that? But my mother just spent ten days in the hospice care center on bed rest to regulate her meds. Anyone would be weak and need time to improve. Of course, she is in hospice care because she's failing. My mother's confusion, her frailty, her more frequent spells of lethargy, the way she gasps for breath—this morning it feels as if I've been irresponsible in delaying a nursing home decision. But how do I know the future? Who am I to be making these decisions? The private care she's getting now will deplete all her money in a year. What if she lives longer than that? Could she end up at that first horrid place? Am I delusional that she'll live a year? Is six months more likely? How much longer will she know anything about anything? "Yes," I say into the faces of the hospice women. I get in the car to cry in private.

It's nine o'clock that night when Aliesa calls. We've know each other's mothers since the times when they would come visit Gainesville. I would play poker with Aliesa's mother and Aliesa would take nature walks with mine. Now our mothers live in the same hall in this same extended care facility, as it is called, and we share a sort of custody of them. She has dinner with her mother each Thursday and always checks in on mine. Tonight she is most excited to report how improved my mother is. This is terrible news. My gut twists and once again, for another time today, I feel a narrowing of vision, a detachment from full consciousness. I lean against my pillows so if I actually faint it won't hurt anything.

Aliesa blithely recounts how my mother asked her to refill the bird feeders, offered her butterscotch candies, and asked about her plans to move in with her girlfriend. She was charming and appropriate. Aliesa is so happy to tell me the good news. I am wracked. I've had it all wrong. She will improve. And I'm thinking of dumping her in a nursing home years before it's necessary. I am evil. An evil daughter in the most stereotyped of ways.

I tell Aliesa all this. I cry, yell, whine, and make her feel bad for telling me my mother is doing well. She adds things to her report.

"Well, Yvonne was unsteady. She couldn't remember what she had for dinner. She hadn't brushed the back of her head and hair was sticking up every which way." She makes me laugh. Then we laugh at ourselves for laughing about my dying mother. Here we are again in this motherland of topsy-turvy where anyone listening in would be appalled by us.

Why do I have to figure this out? It is unfigurable. But so far all the timing for everything has worked out as if I did know the future. Each of my lists, of my preparations, has been of use at just the right time. At first, as I started to plan or, perhaps more accurately, intrude on my mother's life, she would become angry, rightly so. We had no experience, the two of us, as adults, of caretaking each other. And I was too bossy and it was too soon. But now she is beyond noticing. There is only me. The power struggles are over. And I am left alone to decide. Tonight I decide I'll laugh with Aliesa, moments after almost fainting, about the upside-downness of our lives.

But still I yearn to know something, anything. Is this the end? A few days ago the hospice people thought it was. They called in a special nurse to sit with her—a sort of death watch. An hour later my mother woke up and wanted to get out of bed, get dressed, and go eat lunch. Which she did. Is this a time of setback that she'll recover from although at a new, less able level? Or is this the start of a cascade to the end? I want to know. The hospice people say things like "lung disease rollercoaster" and "she always surprises us." Of course she does. My mother survived the Blitz. She escaped the dreariness and poverty of postwar London by finding an American military man to marry. She has always looked out for herself. But that is my job now. And survival can't be the goal anymore.

Aliesa and I end our conversation by chatting a bit about our other lives separate from our mothers' as if we have them. I hang up and pull out a yellow pad. I'm going to redo the figures. If she's doing this well, perhaps I can cancel the night shift of private care. To give the budget flexibility I make up that she'll live two more years. She has about $100,000 in savings. My father's air force pensions come to $4,000 a month. Her long-term health care insurance pays $160 a day for one more year. Her rent is $4,000 a month. Twenty-four-hour private care comes to $174,660 a year. If I cut that in half by canceling the night shift, her money would last more than two years. This could work. If she can make it through the night without falling with just the regular staff checking in on her.

I arrive at seven in the morning to become my mother's private care person for the next nine hours. I've taken extra pain meds to prepare. My purpose is to gather information. Can I drop the night shift? Can I avoid sending my mother to a nursing home? I don't say this to Kimberly, who has been there all night. It means less work for her. She has two young children. I can't think about that. Kimberly is sitting outside the room with her celebrity magazines. She gives me the report. "Miss Yvonne has hardly slept. She had me dress her at two so she'd be ready for your visit and then said I had to wait outside the room. I've been checking in." We roll our eyes. She gathers her stuff and leaves. To me, this sounds promising. I open the door.

My mother is in her big chair reading the paper. She right away reports the news of the day to me—flooding in Tennessee, looking for bodies. Terrible, we both say. Three minutes later she repeats the report with the same, fresh sense of horror. You just said that, I say. Usually I don't, but I so want her to do well today. "Well, it's important," she retorts. Who can argue with that? I don't know whether to put this exchange on the yes or no list for her being on her own at night.

Janisse, part of the regular night staff, comes in on her way off shift and kisses my mother's cheek and adjusts her oxygen and pats her hand and says she'll be back tomorrow night. She pats my shoulder as she leaves. "I take good care of Miss Yvonne in the night, don't you worry." Definitely a yes moment. Except that my mother wants to know why that woman is so affectionate to her. "I've never seen her before in my life."

Mother wants to go to breakfast for the first time in weeks. We exchange her room oxygen for the portable tank that she doesn't remember she needs. Then she gets up on her own and walks to the door with her walker. I have to rush after her. Until today she's had to be pushed in a wheel-chair. She's steadier than I've seen in many months. I call for her to stop.

"Don't you want to take your teapot with you?" This has been her routine for the past year. She takes her teapot and cozy to the dining room, and they make her tea for her.

"What you mean?"

"Don't you want a cup of tea? They'll make it for you."

"They will? Oh, that would be lovely."

At least she remembers the pleasure of a cuppa.

We sit in the lobby (or living room as it is called) and wait with the other early birds for the signal—the lights being turned on in the dining room. She engages with the other residents in charming and appropriate ways. While she and another lady lean over the paper and whisper together about an article, I review. She didn't remember about the portable oxygen that she's used for over two years, but she did walk all the way down the hall without stopping or get-ting more short of breath than usual. Pretty thrilling.

I don't join her and George and Martha at their table for breakfast, despite their protests. I say I've already eaten. I want my mother to do things on her own. And eight hours is a long time to spend every second together. In the past we'd get snippy with each other after about an hour. These days I can stay genial for longer, but my mother can't. I get her settled in and then go sit in the main lobby, where there's an Internet connection.

I don't plan on being gone as long as I am, but I can't look away from the woman who is just back from her morning walk. She glows with skinny old lady health under her sa-fari hat. Her bright pink capris with palm trees machine-embroidered around the cuffs match the sun-faded pink baby stroller she's pushing. Inside is an old, fat chihuahua. It has a neon pink harness. It snuffles and digs into the pro-tective screen. The receptionist chats with the lady and with the dog. I watch and estimate how long it will be before this woman's family is searching out nursing homes for her. I decide it'll be a stroke, probably within a year. She nods over at me, and I can tell she's older than the dyed red hair suggests. I adjust my estimate to six months. A man comes up beside her, one of those tall ones who teeter on skinny legs. He's using a golf club as a cane. Heart attack within six weeks. We smile at each other. Not for a moment do I think I'm a horrible person.

It's been too long. I hurry back and peek in at the dining room. My mother is not there. I go in and inquire. Martha says my mother said she'd forgotten something in her room. George, with his failing eyesight, hadn't noticed she was gone. I power my wheelchair down the hall way too fast for this place. My mother isn't in her room. She hasn't been on her own in two months, and I've lost her. If I was a real private care person, I'd be fired. Where could she be? I look up and down the hall. I see her back just as she's turning into the dining room. How did I miss her? I realize she's been to the hall bathroom. Which means she got up on her own and found the bathroom and came back. Big checks in the yes column.

I go to see her. She has attitude that I wasn't there to help her. Too bad. This is working out really well. I was smart to plan to do this. But it's still not yet nine, and my body is already feeling the wear.

After breakfast I convince my mother to get back in bed and put her feet up. "You know, like the hospice doctor said you should." She loves the hospice doctor, who is from England and will do anything if I say the doctor said she should. Again, I don't think I'm a horrible person when I lie. Needs must. I put my own feet up on her chair. When she falls right to sleep, I wander the halls calling friends and looking at writers' blogs and wishing that I were writing. I could be. I pull out the yellow pad I added to my bag this morning, find a pen, click it on, put it back, and instead play word games on my phone.

My mother sleeps until almost lunch, but I remember that she has been up most of the night. I hover as she moves to the side of the bed. This is when she'll be the most unsteady. She swings her legs to the side of the bed, holds in place, and then pulls her walker to her and stands just like the physical therapist taught her. She's off to the bathroom and then partway out the door. I rush after her with a brush. She no longer cares about bedhead, but I know the old her would be appalled, so I honor who she used to be. Once again she makes it down the hall without having to stop and rest on the strategically placed benches. I join her and George and Martha, "the Washingtons," as she and I call them, for lunch. They make a big deal about how she's back in her regular seat. When she's using a wheelchair instead of the walker she has to sit on a different side of the table. It's closer to Martha, who can't hear very well, so that's better. But it's too far from George to help him find things on the table. Today she hands him the crackers he likes and moves the salt closer. They have their routines.

And after lunch she wants to go sit on the porch. She walks out there fine, but forgets and sits in one of the chairs that is too low for her to get out of, the ones that seem like such a poor choice for a retirement community. Once again, as she has for three years, she asks if the Spanish moss will hurt the trees. Once again, I explain how epiphytes work. But she remembered that it was called Spanish moss. That's pretty good. Her face gets that gray-skinned, slack look. Let's go back in, I suggest. She thinks that's a good idea and tries to get up. No, I say. Press your button. I'm trying to reinforce that behavior.

"Why?"

"Because they'll come help you."

"They will?"

"Yes."

"Why would they do that?"

"It's their job."

"Oh."

"Have you pressed the button?"

"No."

"Well, press it now."

She does, we wait, nothing happens. Press it again, I say. We wait too long. I go inside and ask if the signal came through. The receptionist looks at her screen. No. I go out and press it myself. I go back in. No, it didn't come through. They have this problem sometimes. They will fix it. So much for me teaching my mother to call for help.

Someone comes out and helps my mother up. She walks to her room, once again, no stops, goes to the bathroom on her own, and gets back in bed and sleeps. At three she's up. I ask her if she wants to go to the Cinco de Mayo party in the living room.

"Might as well." This is the most socializing, most food, most walking, most of everything my mother has accomplished in months. This is such a good day. I know it's probably because she's excited that I'm spending it with her. It isn't sustainable. Still, I'm filling the plus side of my mental columns with check marks.

There are the stereotyped straw hats for everyone. The most of a protest I can manage is not to wear one. The chef has set up a table and demonstrates the making of roasted red pepper quesadillas. There is beer. Thimble-sized portions in plastic medication cups are passed out. A mariachi band plays on the boom box. One of the nurses, a six-foot-plus guy, marimbas through the crowd. Partway through Beckie arrives. She had an appointment close by and wanted to visit. She takes over being attentive to my mother and the ladies to either side of her. I help George figure out what's on the plate that someone has put in his hands.

"That's a quesadilla, which is cheese melted inside a flour wrapper. And there's salsa and sour cream. I'll spread them for you."

While I talk to the staff to arrange for the cutting of my mother's toenails, I notice that my mother keeps asking for more quesadilla and more beer. This is excellent. I go to her room to put the nail appointment for next month on her wall calendar. I'll tell her about it when it's closer to the time. The private care person arrives. She's new. I give her the rundown and introduce her to my mother. Right then, I decide. I call the private care service and say, starting tomorrow no more night shifts until I say otherwise. Screw the nursing home plan. I'll inform the hospice women tomorrow.

When I get back to the party, the dancing nurse says that no one can leave without cutting a rug. I grab my mother's hands. "Let's chair dance, Mother." We swing and sway. The crowd ohhs and ahhs. Then I give Beckie the let's-get-out-of-here eye and hand my mother over to the staff.

At 6:59 p.m. the next night, I call Beckie. "In one minute my mother is on her own. Just thought I'd call and share the panic."

This is not hyperbole. I'm having trouble taking any sort of functional breath. I call Aliesa at home. I know she isn't there. It's Thursday again, so she's having dinner with her mother and has promised to look in on mine. I leave a message.

"Aliesa. Call me with a report whenever it is you get in. And get a cell phone, you Luddite."

At 7:10 p.m. I call the nurses' station. I know this is when Paula is giving report to Andre, who will be on the night shift. We are very polite with each other. Six months ago she ignored a delivery of steroids sitting right there on top of the medicine cart and left my mother gasping for each breath for three days. And left me thinking that steroids were no longer working, which the doctor had told me would be an end stage sign. Despite my efforts, there weren't any consequences or even a change in procedure.

"Paula. This is Sandra, Yvonne Lambert's daughter. She's

on her own tonight, you know. I'm a little nervous about it, so this is my first call."

"Yes, Sandra. I was just telling Andre. They'll be checking in regular." Paula has a lovely, soft voice that comforts me despite her incompetence.

I wait until 7:30 p.m. to call my mother.

"I can't make the TV louder. I haven't watched TV in months. (She watched the night before last. I know because she has a thing for Mark Harmon on *NCIS*.)

"Mother, press the button on your wristband."

"Why would I do that?"

"So the staff can help you figure it out."

"Oh, they wouldn't want to do that."

"Yes, they would. That's their job. They've done it before for you."

"Alright, dear. Talk to you later."

"No, mother. Don't hang up. Press your button now, and we'll chat until they arrive." I want to make sure they do, that the button is working, that my mother remembers how to press it.

Two minutes later someone shows up. I hang up as my mother is explaining her problem. I do not call back. It's time to let whatever happens, happen. I pretend to watch television.

The phone rings. It's my landline so it's not my mother. But sometimes the staff calls me on it. I snatch it up. It's Aliesa. There is no preamble.

"I've got to say she looks more with it than ever. Although I almost didn't go in. I peeked around the corner just to suss it out, you know, and she's sitting in her chair with no pants on. But I went in anyway and she engaged very well. Like she even remembered that you had said that I might come. She said you were worried about her being on her own. I reinforced that she should call for assistance and she waved her wristband in my face. Really, it was amazing how with it she was."

"Except for the sitting there pantless."

"Yeah. I don't know what to say about that."

"Did you mention it?"

"No. I thought it would embarrass her."

We hang up, and I unmute the television. I don't call my mother again, but each time I wake in the night I mark time by how many hours it is until the day shift private care person arrives. At 7:30 a.m. I relax. If they'd found her lying on the floor, they would have called by now. One night down.

Nine days later my mother dies.

THIS IS ABOUT SAVING MY LIFE

Invalicide. The murder of the invalid. Say it with an emphasis on the second syllable: in-valid—the not valid person. From a young age I somehow knew Eskimos (as all the native peoples of Alaska were then called by us white children), for the good of society, put disabled people like me out on ice floes to die. I don't remember ever not knowing this. Now I know that it was an old practice and only some groups did this and not that often. Still, the information resonated in my child mind. Already I understood the culture I lived in and often emulated, with its heroes of hearty white frontiersmen and the self-made rich, was a danger to me. So I grew up to be a productive citizen, a good girl, anything not to be ice floe material or the first killed in an apocalypse—zombie, robot, climate change, or nuclear. And as a child, I read everything available to me about the Holocaust. I am not Jewish. Later, of course, I learned of the Third Reich's Aktion T4 campaign that used doctors to murder hundreds of thousands of disabled people, their own citizens, but as a kid the tug of connection was not understood, but nevertheless profound. This early construction of my worldview was reinforced over the decades and underpins interactions with the medical world. It likely underpins everything.

My non-physically-disabled spouse has heard "the talk"

from me before. Not long ago I had breast cancer surgery. I said if things got complicated, Pam had to be careful. After years of pretending to be siblings, parents, or even the children of our hospitalized loved ones in order to be at their bedsides, we old queers can become giddy from the rightful respect we are now sometimes offered. We forget ourselves. I told Pam that if they tried to get her out in the hall for a private conversation, no matter how concerned or caring everyone was, she had to not let that happen. Instead, she must usher them back to my bedside and make them talk to me directly. I appreciated that despite my dictatorial manner in telling her what she must, should, and had to do, Pam listened without showing concern that I was unduly paranoid. I was ready to pounce on an eye roll or slight smile, but it didn't happen. Despite this, I knew she and I didn't understand the dangers in the same way.

Bill Peace wrote the essay "Comfort Care as Denial of Personhood." He was a wheelchair-using white disability activist and scholar and the author of the Bad Cripple website. The essay is about the time he was hospitalized with a dangerous pressure sore. In the middle of the night, after his family had gone home, a "comfort care" team of medical staff he'd never met showed up in his hospital room and offered to help him die. For many years he never told anyone about that doctor, the one who'd sent everyone else out of the room, the one who listed dependence on care, bankruptcy, poor insurance coverage, and never being able to work again as reasons a life, his life, was not worth living. Bill Peace told the doctor he wanted to live, but the visit left him terrified and then ashamed. When he did write about that night, a friend became annoyed. "He thought what I wrote was counterproductive. I was exaggerating the situation. He told me no one is out to get you and you are going to scare people. I replied people with a disability have every right to be scared." Bill Peace's essay has become part of my personal cosmology of disability.

Early on in the pandemic, Pam returned from taking the dog for a walk. Often, we go together. She reported that when the first neighbor came out of their house, rushed over in a way that startled the dog, and asked where I was and how I was, it confused her. Pam muttered that I was busy. Then on the next block, it happened again, and Pam figured it out. Back in our living room, she hammed it up as she reenacted the interactions. We agreed that I'd been designated the neighbor most likely to die. We laughed together. Another neighbor called. She had extra N95 masks she was taking to the fire station, but could she drop one by first? I managed a voice deadpan enough to say "Sure, thanks" with honest appreciation and without rude chortling.

I have a file of yellowing newspaper clippings about Jack Kevorkian, a pathologist who once said that "self-elimination of . . . crippled lives . . . can only enhance the preservation of public health and welfare." The jagged ripped-out pages of the 1993 *Time* magazine profile are in the file as well. Kevorkian left dead bodies in rusted-out vans, in remote cabins, and sprawled in cars abandoned at the front of hospitals. I've forgotten the name of the woman whose life and death most affected me. Her story has lived inside me for almost thirty years. And it was mostly women Kevorkian left me to mourn. Seventy-eight percent. Many of them disabled. But this woman and I were close to the same age. Her multiple sclerosis and my post–polio syndrome meant we'd both recently given up walking for wheelchairs and paid work for government assistance. My ex-lover, after she became my ex, built me a ramp to my apartment. When her husband split, this woman seemed to have no one. She was left in emotional despair with no way to leave her home even to get food. I became a writer, and she reached out to Kevorkian. He didn't say "Let me build you a ramp." He didn't suggest treatment for depression. He didn't deliver groceries. What he said was, I'm imagining, is that if she could get to him, he had this excellent carbon-monoxide delivery system all set up for her. The woman's ex-husband wouldn't bring her even a box of cereal but was willing to take her on that final trip.

The trouble is that this woman whose death I've carried close, she might not be real. I can't find her anywhere in my research. Sherry Miller, Susan Williams, Esther Cohan, Annette Blackman, Margaret Garrish, and many, so many, others all had MS or some other nonterminal disability. But the details of their lives, as far as I can find facts for, don't match. But it is a fact that this particular story, true or not, is the one I pulled together to remember. A worldview also contains myths and fairy tales created from the twisting together of facts with cautionary tales and terror.

As the pandemic progressed, I took all the precautions I could. I'm not referring to masks, distancing, hand washing, isolation, and cancelling follow-up mammograms and certainly dental appointments. I did all this and more, of course. But for me precautions meant something else. The news leaked of state guidelines that would triage disabled people into oblivion. In response Federal Health and Human Services issued a bulletin that prohibited discrimination on the basis of disability. I printed it out and had it ready by the front door along with my advanced directive.

When living wills first became something hospitals asked you to sign on admission, the list of permissions to withhold treatment, along with terminal disease and persistent vegetative state, included being an "invalid." So, twenty years ago, I wrote my own advanced directive. It includes "At no point is it acceptable to limit, ration, deny, or withdraw medical care due to disability. This would be a violation of my civil rights. In short, and put this on my wristband if you need to, do everything and spare no expense." I highlighted the "do everything" part. I thought of having a lawyer write up some legalese about how they'd been engaged to investigate and then sue a hospital posthumously if anything untoward happened.

I decided this was going too far. I'd actually been in a hospital a few years previously for the first time since I was a child. I was treated with respect. Sure, after I was released I almost died of blood loss because no one would listen to me, but that wasn't about disability but rather general incompetence with a big dollop of old lady ageism. And I thought perhaps the media frenzy, with its click-bait headlines about comorbidities and secret ventilator rationing plans, was making me overwrought.

Emmett Everett was killed by a doctor in a hospital in New Orleans during Hurricane Katrina. He was in the hospital waiting to have fairly routine surgery. Because of the storm, his family wasn't there when a doctor who didn't know him, who I don't think has ever spent even a night in jail, took it on herself to give him a deadly injection of morphine combined with a sedative. He wasn't the only patient who was killed that way, that day, by that doctor. But he was fat like I am. He was paraplegic and used a wheelchair like I do. So he's the one I carry with me.

Disability rights groups were now saying to assemble a packet that you would tie to yourself if taken to the hospital. I don't do that. But I used their advice to make a list and placed it on top of the legal papers. Since we now had a pulse oximeter hanging in the kitchen, I figured I'd have enough early warning to assemble everything. The list included extra phone batteries, a phone charger, a wheelchair charger, photos to personalize the hospital room, and copies of my books to put on display. I learned this last trick from the disability activist Harriet McBryde Johnson, who wrote a collection of essays called *Too Late to Die Young*. She was a white Charlestonian lawyer from one of those "good" families, but it wasn't until the hospital staff knew she was a *New York Times*–level famous author that for the first time in her long life of hospitalizations she sensed that she had become human to them. These new preparations weren't something I talked to Pam about. I worried about not being taken seriously enough. I worried she would take it more seriously than I was comfortable with.

Then I saw the photo of Michael Hickson lying in a hospital bed surrounded by his five children who were laughing with him. The reason he was in the news was because Michael Hickson had been a quadriplegic, a Black man, and had died of COVID after being denied treatment. And his wife had a tape. On it the doctor says they are not going to treat him anymore because "his quality of life—he doesn't have much of one." On the tape his wife then asks for clarification. "Because he's paralyzed with a brain injury, he doesn't have quality of life?" The doctor says, "Correct." A friend of mine looked at the photo of Michael Hickson and his children and said she'd never had five people who loved her like that.

Pam loves me. I'd spent a lifetime proofing myself against being the first one thrown out of the lifeboat, put away in a home, considered a life not worthy of life. I was tired of it, tired of the loneliness. So I showed Pam my preparations. I went over each item and the reasoning behind it. When I reached the extra phone batteries line, she touched the list. When I was in the hospital before, each night she'd plug in my phone for me since the outlets were out of reach. When she broke her leg and had to sit and sleep in the recliner, I faithfully made sure all of her devices remained charged. For both of us, in that moment, this became no longer just a list. Whichever one of us was admitted to the hospital during this lockdown, for whatever reason, for an unknown stretch into the future, the other would not be allowed beside them. Dead batteries would mean no contact. By the end of the list, as I'm explaining why the books were not just me bragging about my writing, we were both shaking. Pam's hand was spread over her face, covering her eyes.

Pam has her own roster of people who influence how she interprets the world. She holds inside her own instructive stories that alert her to danger. They aren't the same as mine, but there must be similarities since my hospital list had hammered into her emotions. I felt terrible. I was ready to take it all back or perhaps make a joke about being a drama queen. Pam took my hand. She said, "You always have a plan, don't you? It's how you survive, isn't it? I don't mean emotionally, I mean actually." She looked down the list. "If it comes to this, take my iPad with you. And a copy of our marriage certificate." She reached for the pen and added to the now shared list.

WRITING WHILE HIGH

I have chronic pain. The gut-it-out method was my management strategy until I finally, in my sixties, decided that was inane. Perhaps the older-equals-wiser trope isn't a stereotype. So I said yes to some of the various narcotics that doctors now routinely pushed since somewhere along the way in my life, the medical world had mandated that no pain should be suffered.

The first pill was always effective and quite lovely. But the second one, always, left me desperately nauseated. I'd twist over from my wheelchair and brace my forearms on the toilet seat until my guts ached and acid burned my throat. I'd shiver. Sometimes I'd hallucinate stick figures dancing along the baseboards. Pain was preferable and interfered less than these drugs in the management of my life.

Then my state permitted medical marijuana. I'd stopped smoking pot in the 1970s because of paranoia and anxiety. But they said this wasn't your grandparents' marijuana. (By "grandparents" they meant people my age.) It was expensive not just for the actual drug but also for all the licensing and required appointments, and you can be sure that Medicare did not pay for it. I'd hand over a stack of cash to a young woman who showed up at my door with a brown paper bag. She was guarded by a hulk of a guy with his arms crossed over his chest. The exchange had a nostalgic thrill of the illicit. And the drug did diminish the pain to an extent, but then all the reasons I quit using back in the 1970s were there again—anxiety, paranoia, and even more fatigue than I already had.

My physician suggested Gabapentin, which is not considered a narcotic. It wasn't addictive, she said. So I started, small doses building up to bigger ones. I didn't throw up. It worked great for pain. But I was stoned every day in a way that limited my life more than the pain had. Plus, I was not willing to never, ever have an orgasm ever again. So I decided to quit. I dropped my dosage little by little the way you're supposed to and, wow, I felt bad. Electrical shocks sparked all over my skin. I sweated. I was outrageously anxious. I cried and cried. But I gutted it out and after a month that withdrawal from the supposedly not addictive drug was done.

Pain now woke me up every night. Which for aging bladders is helpful in that it keeps us from peeing a little in the bed, which can happen if we're sound sleepers. When I had been a sound sleeper, I'd have dreams where I searched and searched for a bathroom, but they were all inaccessible. The door would be too narrow, a sink would block the toilet, or there'd be a step. Finally, I'd wake up desperate to pee. So inaccessibility had helped me to not wet the bed. But sometimes, in my dream, I'd find a bathroom that worked, transfer onto the seat, and let go with a sigh. Which meant I peed the bed. Which was a disorienting Mobius twist of access and using a wheelchair in waking life. But that didn't happen for me anymore because pain kept my sleep drifting just under and into consciousness. I'd shift and search for a better position. I'd sit up. I'd lay back down. Then I'd be stern with myself. Ignore the pain.

But another layer of the getting smarter with age must have activated. Instead of counting sheep, I started counting pain. I'd begin with my hands. The right thumb hurt at its base, the left one didn't. Some nights both wrists felt as if they had tightening cuffs around them. The right shoulder was like bread dough on the skin's surface, spongy and numb. Inside, deep and twisting, was a razor blade. By the time I reached my back with the catch under the left scapula, I was often asleep. But if not, I moved on to counting the left hip, which was not firmly settled in its socket anymore, which made it chronically inflamed, and if I moved a certain way, a way that I could never anticipate, it jerked loose. After all these years of ignoring pain or being told it didn't exist, paying note of it soothed me. Parts of my brain that had been on alert for a lifetime relaxed. It helped, but I would still hurt and sleep was still thin.

Right now, two years later, I'm high on Gabapentin again. A friend told me how she takes one occasionally for back pain, and I literally smacked my own self up the side of the head because I hadn't thought of that before. Older and wiser had failed me. And I blamed my all-or-nothing brain. It had insisted that occasional pain relief would make me notice more when I was in pain, ruin my ability to deal with pain, and make me sad about being in pain. The logic of this is wrong. That's not how it works. I wonder what else I think this way about?

I took three hundred milligrams of Gabapentin last night. There is wonder in the way pain falls off my body in waves. And I sleep great and don't hurt or at least I don't care that I hurt and I love it so much. My new regimen is to dose myself once a week or so on a day when I don't have to drive or speak to anyone much. At first, I didn't realize how much I slurred words. Then I listened to an audio recording I made on a "gaby" day. I should have left it up online just for the Cheech and Chong jokes at my expense. I have also learned, the wet way, to set the alarm for two am and then again at five am and each time ask myself if I need to go to the bathroom.

Another worry was about losing a writing day, but I am writing. Not well, but a lot. This is despite the irresistible distractions of emails and Facebook notifications that it seems I must open immediately if I'm high. Or I wander over to TikTok and giggle at the guy from Florida as he becomes a dying air conditioner or fall even more in love with Sharkie and their dragon Cupcake. And then I watch videos of the guy who impersonates dogs and laugh and laugh—I mean, the one where he's just been groomed and jumps in the mud puddle can't be watched often enough. And I add emoji hearts to a lot of friends' posts and write "awwwww" on too many others because I adore everyone right now. When I get up I'm careful of the door jambs because my power chair counts as operating heavy equipment. Once I tuck myself back on the bed and arrange all the pillows, the dog jumps up beside me. We have a long conversation while I scratch that place under her ear and she looks at me with liquid love eyes.

But sometimes I pop the current document to the forefront of the computer screen, and I am back to writing and words just come and come. This is unusual for me. My editing brain usually kicks in before I've written a single word. But it seems to have gone on a little vacation. Probably to a sentence diagraming conference or grammar convention or maybe to a meditation retreat for uptight, controlling cerebral cortexes. I can hope. I make a plan of how to use the drugged-up days efficiently. I'll plan new writing on the moderately wasted day and revisions the rest of the week.

I still hurt on the other days. And I do get sad as the drug wears off and pain reassembles over my body. But at night I count pain and it still helps me sleep. And these days I have a set of exercises for my rotator cuff problem, as it's been labeled. What with all those years of crutch walking and manual wheelchair pushing, I'm like old athletes with their wraps, ice packs, and physical therapy appointments. Actually, I am an old athlete. Perhaps it's time to rest on my laurels. I don't know what that means, but since I'm at the in-my-seventies level of smart now, I might figure it out.

BATTLE STATIONS

The needle appears thick and six inches long as it slides through shifting ripples of white and lakes of black. This is what my breast looks like in the magnification of the ultrasound monitor. The tip approaches the first mass to be biopsied. A radiologist, a tech, a resident, and an unidentified someone else crowd around and over me, and claustrophobia has me looking through a crook of an elbow, curve of a waist, the sideways shift of a hip in an attempt to find my wheelchair. They've moved it out of reach. Evasion or escape isn't possible. I remind myself that neither the needle nor the mass is actual size.

The radiologist gives directions to the resident guiding the needle. The mass slips under the needle. The radiologist shoulders the resident away and takes his place. The needle pulls back and tilts down. We all watch the screen as the edge of the mass dents and strains against the tip and then rebounds as the needle enters. Breaths are released. I hear a snip. And another when an incandescent marker is left at the scene.

"Just in case there's surgery. It will guide their way," she says.

This is the first needle.

We were a military household. A family joke about illness was my father saying that one morning, for fifteen minutes, he'd had the twenty-four-hour flu. I was the oldest child, and I thrived in a culture where failure was unacceptable and all objectives could be accomplished. My first crutches were wooden, eighteen inches long, and tucked into my armpits. A metal band attached to my leg braces circled my waist just above the diaper.

While my father was at work, perhaps managing the immense complexities of support for the movement of personnel around the world, I learned how to lift myself up from falls, developed an effective, controlled tumble down stairs, created a technique to launch myself up into the school bus, and mapped out clandestine routes to avoid the school hallways where kids chanted "crip, crip."

When I was eleven, pantyhose became affordable. From what I could tell from the picture on the package, they would work to protect my skin from the friction of leather pads and the bite of metal edges. My mother wouldn't pay for them. She said I was too young, and she was right to suspect I also wanted them for the adult sexy femininity I thought they would confer. But I've guarded my personal autonomy from before I had the words, so starting with the first dollar bill that fell out of a birthday card from a distant relative, I've been a saver. I used babysitting money to buy the pantyhose for myself. Mission executed.

I'm on a stretcher in nuclear medicine naked except for the surgical gown. The lights are dimmed. The lumpectomy happens today, but first, any moment now, a blue dye will be injected into my breast. It will reveal which are my sentinel nodes, the ones they'll remove from my armpit and test for metastasis. No one uses that word. Instead they say "Check for involvement." During a previous office visit the resident (a different one) winced as he said this part would involve discomfort. The surgeon's expression was more dramatic when she allowed that it would sting. Just now the anesthesiologist said it would hurt—no expression.

Once I'm positioned on the table, a staff person settles

beside me and takes my hand. In this moment she has no other duties. Back in the shadows of the machine, someone else is handling the procedure. This means the corporate entity she works for, the one that provides her a salary, health insurance, and vacation days and is perhaps contributing to a 401K, gifting a holiday bonus, or allowing family leave and is on the hook for their portion of social security, Medicare, unemployment taxes, and workers comp, is paying her to sit quietly beside me. This is going to be bad. The other person in the room nods at the hand-holder, who says to me, "Just five seconds. It will be over in five seconds." She grips my hand and holds her own breath. This is the second needle.

"Sturdy as a bull," was how I used to describe myself. And when I said "bull," I'd bulk up my wide-from-crutch-walking shoulders and swing them back and forth as if I were a football player. Sometimes I'd make huffing sounds. After the flurry of orthopedic surgeries that ended when I was five and besides a maybe-once-a-decade head cold, I was never ill. Disability was different from illness. Disabled was different from fragile.

Within a month after the second needle, my breast swells to the size and consistency of a bowling ball. The surgical resident (a different one) says he can numb the area, but that would take multiple punctures and he only needs one quick stick to get a culture. I don't know yet that it will never be "one quick stick." He is unsuccessful, repeatedly, in finding any pus or blood. He calls it a hematoma and says to use a heating pad. The medical team calls it a postsurgical abscess, is hesitant to proceed with radiation, and refers me back to the surgeon. She sweeps into the room. She gives the only-one-stick speech. I fall for it again. I grip the railings and push with all my strength to remain immobile as the needle plunges. She moves it this way and that. She pulls it almost out, changes the angle, and goes deep again. Technically, it is only one stick. Tears drip from my chin and land close to her hand. But she is successful. She slaps the syringe of pus into her resident's (a different one's) hand and leaves. My breast is infected. Antibiotics are added to my regimen. The area deflates.

The rawness of my breast is to be expected. The bright pain of peeling flesh becomes routine. But the blister that bubbles along the incision is something else. The radiation oncology team says the abscess is back and sends me across the street to the surgical clinic. A resident (a different one) comes in with a needle already in his hand. He has a medical student with him. He looks at the ultrasound. He says he can't see any pockets of infection. He wants to try anyway. He reads me a list of risks and slurs over the part about nerve damage because, he says, the breast has no significant nerves. The female medical student and I give each other a look. I'm the old lesbian in the room and so probably have the most expertise, but I decide not to give him a lecture on female erogenous zones. I wonder if my breast will ever be an erogenous zone again. He gives the one-stick spiel. I fall for it again. He sticks me four times and pain overwhelms me. He finds nothing, which he'd predicted. The exam table was too high for me to transfer onto, so I'm in my wheelchair. He's draped me in a haphazard way and now the blood has covered my belly and soaked into my waistband. It will never come out. The pants are a lovely peach and lightweight and made of cotton that looks like linen. They were on sale.

Suddenly, I'm sobbing and hissing at him about how he's ruined my pants. It is an absurd sort of anger. He whispers to the medical student, who goes out to the hall. He packs his supplies and exits as soon as the medical student comes back with what I name the "nurse for criers." She's the one they call when a patient loses it. She empathizes by being angry about my pants with me and uses words like "sucks" and "crappy day." I am soothed and feel manipulated at the same time.

The pain emoji scale is also absurd. My personal pain scale is made up of pain I can ignore, which is most pain. Then there's pain I have to pay attention to, which besides limiting my movements and well, hurting, annoys me. I've been dismissive of pain, mine and other peoples. It's a paradox. Polio is said to diminish the body's ability to use its own natural pain relievers, endorphins and such, which causes pain to be felt more intensely. You'd think those of us with polio would be especially fond of narcotics and demand them for even the slightest of bodily insults, but many of us are the opposite. It makes sense. Since childhood my expressions and complaints of pain, especially of supposedly everyday pain like cavity fillings, spankings, shots, cramps, or the cold, have been gaslit with disbelief and derision. Once my mother paid attention to how after a flight, I screamed from ear pain. She took me to a doctor. He smirked and implied I was playing her. She was embarrassed to have taken his time. So we, I, became known not for a decreased pain tolerance, but an increased one. But the pain from the radiation and the abscess and the needles wears at me. It is pain I can't pretend not to be having. It makes me lose track of conversations. People notice. Being caught out like this embarrasses me.

The next day I'm back at the surgeon's office. A resident (the same one) pokes his head in the door and jokes around about how he doesn't have a needle with him today. I don't joke back. I mutter "twerp" mostly under my breath. He leaves. Another resident (a different one) comes in and looks at my uncovered breast. "Unfortunate." he says. "You're a nice lady. This shouldn't have happened to you." I'm furious at myself that they think I'm a nice lady. If I'd been doing this right, I should be known as a harridan, a hag, a harpy. I should have a reputation that proceeds me, a bad one. They should be scared to see me coming, not me them. How did I become this weakling? When did I acquiesce?

My life has, by necessity, because of disability among

other reasons, made me the opposite of weak, but in dribs and drabs of small assaults, I've retreated. The surgeon arrives. She doesn't mess around with needles. The scalpel cuts. It doesn't hurt, and my skin spreads open to reveal layers of pink, white, and yellow covered in streamers of red blood. I'm reminded of camellia blooms. The lab results say I have the same infection as before.

But it has been an effective strategy for me to seem nice, which means perceived as compliant, which I often wasn't. When I was a kid, in an attempt to correct the bone torsions in my lower legs, a parent came into my bedroom every night and attached a metal contraption between my ankles. They were instructed to tighten it two twists past when I said it hurt. I'd pretend to sleep until after the second time the door opened and light fell over me. My fingers were just strong enough to release the bolt. At dawn, I'd twist it back. It was a successful strategy to getting and going my own way that I still use. That way no one gets a piece of me.

But these days I'm losing pieces of myself anyway. Sometimes actual pieces. The infection continues. I need to change my tactics. So I follow instructions. I learn how to use an ice-tea-spoon-length Q-tip to stuff long ribbons of cotton gauze deep into the channels of the abscess. In the evenings, I pull it out and stuff in more. It helps to imagine myself a field medic packing a gut wound and radioing for a helicopter, trying to be heard over the artillery fire. I send iPhone photos of my breast to the surgeon's office. More antibiotics are prescribed. There are office visits and more residents, most of whom are eager to take me to surgery for "a little cleanup." I make sure they know I think they are ignorant for forgetting that my radiated skin will dissolve from not much more than a hard look. One of them calls me "Honey," and I make him regret it. The surgeon talks about how long this healing will take, having patience through plateaus, that time will tell. But I see the looks that pass between the residents, the surgeon, the nurse, and anyone else crowded into the exam room. I sit among them with my reddened and dented breast exposed and a pus-encrusted stub of cotton gauze hanging down alongside a nipple.

When I was a little kid in the hospital, I remember trying to figure out what terrible thing was going to happen next by noticing looks like these. I imagine my breast concealing a maze of infection-ridden tunnels and that after all this I'll end up with a mastectomy. Early on, before the biopsy, when I misread the mammogram results and thought the masses were much bigger than they were and I'd have to have a mastectomy for sure, I decided I didn't want breast reconstruction. I researched "flat" closures. I reached out to an author friend who'd had one. I found my way to private Facebook groups of flat activists. Trans guys I knew who'd had top surgery, their chests looked great, nothing like some of the photos on the FB pages showing failed flat closure surgeries. I had made lists of the questions to ask. Did the surgical team have experience in this area? What did they do to prevent dog-ears? Did they use a fishtail incision or a VY plasty? In the middle of the night, I turn on the bedside light, find my notes, and rememorize all the terms.

I've never thought of myself as adapting to disability. It has always been a given. I've just lived my life. Getting rid of the metal band around my waist and switching to aluminum crutches was a child's progression through the stages of development. The hand controls installed on the family station wagon when I was fifteen was a rite of passage that was fraught only for my mother, who, like many mothers, panicked at the inherent danger of her girl child loose in the world. Switching to using a wheelchair was the smart move for continued mobility. But illness is not the same as disability. (Although I've never yet been ill from cancer, just from the treatments.) Strategies like believing that it's always safest to figure out solutions on my own and that gutting through pain is a good choice aren't as effective as they once were.

I go to my family doctor and ask for help. She studies my computerized medical chart. The postsurgical infection is not listed anywhere. She types it in as a diagnosis and emphatically hits the enter key. My reality of these past months now officially exists. Just that makes me stronger. She suggests a specialized wound care center and arranges with the surgeon for that to happen. There they spread anesthetic cream over the area and wait before they touch it. I never knew such a thing existed. They poke, measure depths and widths, and ask me, more than once, if they're hurting me. This is the first time I've been asked that. I want to say that it's the first time ever in my life, but that seems impossible.

There are no big changes. The regimen of packing is adjusted, but still each day, twice a day, no matter if I'm at home or on a book tour, I grit my teeth and push the strips of cotton into my breast. I get the job done. Antibiotics are added again. The wound care doctor also looks worried and says if it heals, it will take a long time. But I go each week, and each week the treatments are reevaluated. The pain diminishes. The size of my breast diminishes. My bra, sheets, and towels are littered with sloughs of radiation-burnt skin. Under the soft, fresh skin the abscess fills in and the bruising reabsorbs. It was June when I had the surgery. At Thanksgiving the wound care doctor says, "When you first came in, I was pretty sure you would need a mastectomy. I don't think that anymore."

The wound care doctor has said out loud what I decoded from secret looks months ago. I am affirmed. I am affirmed that it is not always dangerous to ask for help. I know now that to be ill is not to be fragile or to have failed. Not everything is a mission. And pain, enduring it, has shaped me and has been doing so for a long time. In March my wound is declared healed. The surgeon and I finally sign off on each other.

Four years later it's time for what I used to call, before cancer, my yearly routine mammogram. I don't call anything routine anymore. And this mammogram shows a disturbance in the field. I'm pushed again to the medical front lines, but this time I'm seasoned. The staff person escorting me to the changing room is excited because just that morning the masking requirements have ended. I ask her to put one on anyway. She won't. I tell her to leave the room, she does, and I'm overly triumphant about intimidating a very young, white, sweet-faced woman. Before I even get home, a message arrives that the results are hinky and I need to come back. I call right away thinking they'll get me in that day, because making someone who has had breast cancer wait to find out if there's a reoccurrence, if it has become metastatic, which means fatal, would be cruel. I call the appointment desk, I message my physician, I reach out to someone I know who is a corporate muckety-muck at the hospital, but my appointment still has to wait for a month.

I know when a struggle isn't worth it, and instead I strategize for the future. As with most of us who have had a questionable mammogram lead to surgery and radiation, the assumed results are always cancer. No logic, statistics, or facts will change the emotions of that, but still I research. I do learn that since the hinkiness found is in the other breast that a second primary cancer is a possibility. Which is not a metastasis. So there's that.

By the end, all those years ago, my original surgeon and I were done with each other. So I ask my physician to recommend another breast surgeon just in case. Metastatic or primary, this time I'm getting both breasts whacked off. I pull out my old research on flat closures. A month is a long time. I watch many episodes of "Say Yes to the Dress." I note that one very flat-chested woman (they never say she had cancer) looks glamourous in a high-necked bodice of intricate lace.

An architectural distortion is what the second mammogram report calls it. The wavy lines on the screen pull together as if something is tugging on them. An unseen something. "Given your history" a biopsy, this one computer guided, is recommended.

"Computer guided" means the radiologist and her resident are across the room behind a screen that I can't see sending computer-generated coordinates to the twelve-gauge needle locked in above my breast, which is trapped, compressed between the plastic plates. Every other time a needle has punctured my breast, someone was close enough that I could, theoretically, backhand them. I had not known how much the possibility of that soothed me until now, when it is not possible.

But there is no pain. No pain at all. Even the compression is only uncomfortable. Even the tiny lidocaine needles don't sting, even as the resident pushes them deeper and deeper. The anesthetic itself doesn't burn. The thick needle lowering deep into my breast is strange to watch but not painful. Perhaps it's this absence of hurt, along with the memory of pain, that overwhelms me into almost crying. The nurse hovering beside me offers her hand to hold. I take it, but then I'm fine. I push it away. I ask many questions. The needle is rotated, and twelve times, at each station of the clock, it pauses and snatches tissue. I hear suction and see pink blood and yellow clumps mix into clear liquid and move through a tube.

On my way out the nurse says what a good patient I was. It makes me mad. I wonder what would have made me a bad patient. If I'd cried? If I'd thrashed? She holds open the door for me. I pause and look at her. I say, What choice was there? You had my breast trapped in a machine with a needle in it. At least she's not smiling at me anymore. It only takes three days to find out, that this time, no cancer cells are detected.

ALLIGATOR PROTOCOLS

Yellow with brown stains, muted aqua, green, and red (actually more pink these days but we remember it as red)—all of our aged kayaks are launched and my wheelchair is secured under the roof of a picnic pavilion. Beckie, Madeline, and I have made this trip into the Myakka wilderness area, the last time twenty years ago. Pam has not. I go over the alligator protocol. Of all of us, I am the least scared of alligators. Madeline, the five generations of Florida native, is next. Then Beckie. And then my wife, Pam, whose fear of them has ruined trips for her in the past. I'd offered her the option of not coming this time both for her sake and selfishly thinking that might be easier on all of us. She insisted. I know it will help that there aren't just the two of us. And I know my job is to be calm, fearless, and present a clear strategy.

Myakka River State Park doesn't have the most alligators I've ever wandered among, but they have the biggest. And after the last bridge, past the forest, the river becomes a creek bounded by grassy banks and sandbars. In places it's not much wider than a kayak. And that's where the twisty portion of the trip begins. I go over the game plan, mostly for Pam.

Around each tight curve is the chance of an alligator, maybe a behemoth, baking itself on the shore, I say. This has never happened for us, but if it does decide to startle, the ancient instinct tells it to head for water, I say. They are not attacking when they do this, but the creek is narrow and shallow, and in some places the alligator won't be able to sink and might bump our boats. I'll go first. If I signal, make sure there is space between us. Don't bunch up.

We're ready. I put my paddle down to push into the current. An alligator head coalesces out of the murk alongside, almost under, the boat, inches from where my hand is wrapped around the shaft. It stares at me, holding in place with its body too deep to see so the head seems to float free. It keeps staring in what I'm making up as dreadful intent. In my own ancient instinctual way, I am freaked the fuck out. I jerk my hand away and swallow a yelp, but not well enough that the other kayakers don't look over. I keep holding the paddle high and pretend to untangle the paddle leash. The alligator head dematerializes as it drops back into the depth of the river. I press a hand to my chest and will my heart to slow, but Pam notices and tilts her head in the way that means she's asking if anything is wrong. I smile back and pretend I'm scratching my collarbone. In the meantime, I evoke the necessary Florida survival fantasy that when an alligator sinks from view, they have disappeared into another realm. Still, I only let the paddle blade skip over the surface until we are under the bridge and into the wilderness area.

The live oaks still lean over the banks. The resurrection fern along the branches is green and unfurled from a recent rain. That bodes well for getting through to the lower lake. I'm remembering that last trip we'd had to hump the kayaks over a long buildup of sand just before the creek entered open water. It had exhausted me. My arm strength gave out on the return trip, and I'd had to rest in eddies, over and over, before I could make it back to our campsite. I'd made Beckie sing to me to distract from the pain. I feel the memory in my shoulders. And then the memory of grief joins in.

That was perhaps the first time I was old enough to think I'd never get to do something again.

Since then I've thought this many times about many activities. Not all these last times made me sad, and some were to be celebrated. I've aged out of needing pap smears and routine colonoscopies, and hygienists no longer shame nag me about flossing. I'd suggested to the doctor doing that last pap smear that she should have provided noise makers, confetti, and a balloon drop from the ceiling. The ability to eat pizza and garlic rolls together without consequence ended many years ago but so what. On the trip to Alaska for my sixty-fifth birthday, Pam and I celebrated with a guided overnight camping kayak trip. Paddling into Kachemak Bay bordered by glaciers was glorious, and it had also been when I decided that was the last time I would voluntarily sleep on the ground. And sometimes, I'm wrong. I'm making this trip into the wilderness again or at least trying.

Once we reach the end of the forest and the beginning of the many sandbars, I take point. My technique is to approach each turn as far as I can from the outside edge. I lean forward to get the earliest possible view into the curve of the upcoming bank but alligator or no, I announce our arrival. "Hello, just us. Coming on by. Don't bother yourself." I use a conversational voice and am loud enough so we're not a surprise, but since I don't know if alligators hear humans, mostly I say it to keep myself relaxed. I'm still spooked from that alligator I haven't told anyone about. It's a new sensation.

Friends in their eighties have commented on experiencing anxiety for the first time or a new quality of anxiety as they age. Is it happening to me? Perhaps it will lead to more empathy for the alligator fearful. I watched an interview with Alice Walker about her upcoming compilation of fifty years of journals. She was, patronizingly I thought, asked if she still had adventures. After what I took as an annoyed pause, she replied, "What makes an adventure is that it's new. So, yes." A variation on newness is returning to the same place with a body and a mind that has changed and is changing.

At the first twisty-section alligator sighting, I raise my arm above my head. But that allows the current to throw me toward the bank, so I drop my hand to grab up the paddle. The paddle clangs against the boat. Each quick stroke splashes water and skitters over the surface. My technique is inefficient and awkward. This is not the silent glide I'd imagined. I don't even have time to throw a judgmental glance behind me in case whoever is next has followed too close. As they always do, the alligator seems to follow me with its eyes without moving its head. And then, right away, it's time to lean forward and spy out the next curve. No one calls out from behind and I don't hear the distinctive long splash of an alligator launching itself into the water. So we're good.

When I lived in Norway, the brag was that their coastline, if stretched out, would wrap around the Earth two and half times. The one-inch stretch of blunt squiggles on our map are not representative of reality, so I don't know how far I travel on high alert. All the alligators we pass ignore us, including the easily-thirteen-footer that causes me to hold my breath as if that is some sort of magic calming spell. Finally, the banks drop below eye level, and I can see open water ahead. The path straightens and we are close to where the creek pours out through the mudflats and into the lower lake. The water stays high enough for the boats to float free and finally our kayaks have room to come alongside each other. Everyone, by which I mean Pam, looks okay, even excited. I lean back into the seat and rest my paddle over my lap. We are the only humans here.

We hear the birds first as flocks announce themselves to rise and fly to their next perch of mud and shallow water. This is how it always is here. All the birds, all around us. Elegant black-necked stilts strutting, gray willets who flash bright patterns whenever they spread their wings, roseate spoonbills swinging their beaks back and forth in the shallows, and floating circles of white pelicans fish in the cooperative way that they do. Sandhill cranes bugle overhead. They are the loudest despite how high they are in the sky because of the tracheas coiled in their chests. The tracheas would be two feet long if stretched out.

Other paddlers often keep paddling until they reach the famed Deep Hole where alligators congregate in massive numbers, but I know my limits. Not of alligators, but of traveling over open water with no wind protection. We find a sandbar without a lounging reptile and paddle hard at it so our bows stick despite the current pulling at us. Some of us stand partway to test the sand and mud mix. No one's legs sink to their knees. No sandals are sucked off and lost forever in the mud. They decide it's safe to move their full weight out of the kayak to stand upright, stretch, pee. I worm my wet pants down just enough, hang my butt over the edge of the kayak, and do the same. We have lunch in the middle of the bird cacophony. An alligator swims by and looks at us on the sandbar. It continues on into the lake.

As we secure our trash for the return trip, Madeline says she'll go first on the way back. Pam offers to take turns with her. We all look at Pam. She shrugs. Beckie says there must be something to that immersion therapy thing. I still don't mention my moment of alligator terror. As we paddle home, I hold up the rear. I'm careful not to bunch. Despite the current, I'm able to keep up. I don't understand why, except that there's an excitement and energy in being unchained from responsibility.

After showers, after anti-inflammatories, after naps, after dinner, we play dice games in the cabin we've rented instead of camping like we used to and revel in our adventure. Each individual alligator's size, closeness, and whether it's mouth was open or if it twitched a foot is discussed. Pam announces that from now on any moment of fear will be judged against this trip. I confess about the floating head that stared at me with such purpose and accept the deserved teasing. Later, owls hunt just outside, Madeline serves the apple pie, and I appreciate the ease of moving in a wheelchair while I bring plates to the kitchen. Each of us imagines new adventures—a trip to Italy, a road trip out West, kayaking the Colorado River, through the San Juan Islands, on the fjords of Norway. We've adapted ourselves to this next stage of exploration with hotels instead of tents and extra days for a slower pace. We have to save more and for longer or choose closer trips, but what does it matter. I don't say it out loud, but I'd made sure I had the bowline attached today. My secret backup plan for the loss of paddling strength had been to have the rest of the group take turns hauling me upstream. It seems these days part of my adventuring is to risk the embarrassment of needing unplanned help.

That night I fall asleep in a relatively comfortable bed, next to a private bathroom, in a cabin with a full kitchen and a choice of heat or air conditioning. I remember leaning on the kayak's backrest to watch an undulating line of white pelicans fly low overhead. Their black and white wings spanned nine feet and I could hear the way the air crooned over their surfaces. Most likely I'll never return to that particular place. But this time, twenty years later, I don't mourn. There is only satisfaction. And joy.

OLD. LADY. DABBLER.

OLD.

Age is slippery. When I first started writing, I was forty, which is about twenty-six generations of the mice that rattled around in my kitchen, but no more than a sapling compared to the tulip poplar whose branches hung over the parking space of my basement apartment in Atlanta. I didn't know this, but from the beginning of my writing life it was already too late for me to be considered an "emerging writer." I figured it out when I saw a full-color spread of the winners the National Book Award for debut novelists. (They call it "5 Under 35.") I was fifty-four. If I ever had a debut novel (which wouldn't happen until I was sixty-two), this recognition was off limits. To the literary world, who I was didn't exist.

I don't know why I wasn't a writer earlier, a writer who wrote her first story in crayons or was a reporter for the high school newspaper. All the signs were there. I was never brave enough to risk the disciplinary consequences of being caught with a flashlight under the covers, but I'd read through twilight and as far into the dark as possible. My eyes would ache even the next morning. In elementary school I'd use the open-book-on-top-of-an-open-textbook technique to finish off a Hardy Boys novel during math class. My long division skills still suffer. My first crushes were school librarians, all of them. We had our special time together, since a disabled girl like me wasn't allowed to go to gym class so the principals at all the schools I attended stashed me in the library. It was an odd mix of feeling, again, excluded, alongside the thrill of spending time with books and kind, lovely women. Then there was my extensive collection of bookmarks: lace, wooden, embossed leather, ribbons with beads, and flowers pressed inside plastic. But despite even the classic signs of a writer, which include calling in sick to work to finish reading a novel and managing a bookstore, I didn't write.

But I do know what was happening when I first wrote. The feminist bookstore I worked at immersed me in that 1980s swell of lesbian-feminist publishers, printers, journals, and authors. I worked and played and did social change within a community rich with writers of all sorts, and it was a community that valued our stories as much as, sometimes more than, the craft or skill in telling it. So as untrained as I was, I felt welcome to contribute.

The other factor, the main one perhaps, is that my body changed. I had polio as a baby and had used braces and crutches all my life and that's just how it was and I didn't think much about my body. It was sturdy and skilled and it got me where I wanted to go. It was a stable, unchanging situation. But it did change. What we now know as post-polio syndrome kicked in with its hallmark features of weakness, pain, and fatigue. In many ways, overnight, I became my own stereotyped image of an old person what with the naps, the falls, and the audible groans with each reach, lift, or twist. I had to make changes. I had to, for the first time perhaps, pay attention to my body. And this is when I wrote that first poem, first essay, first story. I tried everything.

This was a hard time in my life. But when I wrote something, anything, I was thrilled. It was an excitement that these words now existed in the world when they hadn't before. And I wanted to show everyone what I'd done in the same way a little kid runs around in a flush of creative glee waving their drawing and shouting "Look, look, look!" until someone slaps it up on the fridge with magnets. The equivalent for me was when journals we sold in our bookstore, such as *Sinister Wisdom* and *Common Lives/Lesbian Lives*, published my work. Then, if you were somehow tracking me from the outside, I went quiet. I didn't publish again for fifteen years.

These days we talk about it sometimes. How, for some of us, our trajectory as writers is delayed. For me there was addiction, abuse, and the drowning confusion of showing up on a campus as the first in my family to graduate high school much less go to college. And I was female and physically disabled. And a lesbian in a time when even the word was unknown to me. So very much creative and emotional energy as well as inexorable hours in a day were used up in negotiating the world under these circumstances. I am not unique. My circumstances are not comprehensive. It is not just some of us. And we are not delayed. Our talent, our skills, our perseverance, and our wild joy in writing are not despite obstacles. They arise from the supposed dead ends and loop-de-loops of our lives.

LADY (White):
Still comfortably clueless about the literary world, I kept writing during those fifteen years. I lived in Florida now. I surpassed the lifespan of an alligator in the wild, survived the menopausal decade, and entered the aging parrot years. This is when I acquired more of the hallmarks of an old lady dabbler. Considering someone just an "old dabbler" wouldn't be the same. Putting the female presentation label in the middle twists the phrase into its pinnacle of disdain.

Every author who came through town, of whatever genre, would look out over their audience and see me, a graying white lady, perched in her wheelchair near the front with an alert, too-eager expression, and sure enough I'd be the first to ask a question, often a banal one. Even as I asked it, I cringed at how predictable it was. But I wanted answers to questions I didn't know the words for, so I asked the obvious—what time of day do you write, do you write directly onto a computer, who are your favorite authors, how does one get an agent. I wanted some elusive-to-me something from these writers and, even in the moment, I could tell how unappealing, perhaps repellent, my raw need was. Later, at home, I'd cry from embarrassment. But I shrugged off the shame, kept writing, and showed up at the next reading. I think there is much about being raised female starting in the 1950s that helps us survive shame.

In the past month a cashier expressed wonder that I grocery shop, a hotel clerk was impressed I travel on my own, and when I opened the door into a taco hut, my skill was commented on. This has happened all my life. So all praise becomes suspect. It meant when I discovered that there were these things called writing workshops you could pay to attend, I noticed right off the patronizing tone in response to my work. But my sense was this time it had more to do with me being a woman, an older woman, than anything about disability. The younger participants' writings received the respect of a more nuanced feedback that assumed a career path forward for their work. Mine did not. I'd look over at their sample pages and the instructor would have written hundreds of words more in the margins than on mine. At the bottom would be long paragraphs of suggestions. Much later, when I started leading workshops myself, I asked more experienced writers for advice. The responses sometimes included variations of "the older women, mostly all they want is to be told how good their writing is. Just praise them and you'll be fine."

DABBLER.
"Old" is accurate. "Lady," sure, no problem. "Dabbler" is the most fraught word in this phrase. As if dabblers don't come

in all ages and in all genders. As if the man who distorted his mouth sideways to faux whisper it during postworkshop socializing at a bar could know the future of the writer he was dismissing or even his own future. A young person learning their craft is not a dabbler but an older person is? "Dabbler" implies lack of skill but more accurately means a lack of success however your slice of the writing world defines it. I mostly write in the literary genre, so success includes prestigious journals, fellowships, and literary awards rather than just book sales and reader popularity. I had to learn all this.

Dabblers are also identified by their ignorance. Those of us who enter the hurly-burly of literary community later in life are strangers in a strange land. We can feel bodychecked by a world where it helps to know someone except we don't know who that is, where we are routinely embarrassed, even humiliated, and where responses can seem elitist or snobby. I didn't know the language. "Slush," "partial," "a good rejection," and "to be solicited" had new meanings. I didn't know that when an agent said my work was "quiet," it was her using a kinder term than "boring."

I had more success. I began to "know" people, and I cloaked myself in the armor of my publications and awards. I came to like it when someone at a writer gathering made dabbler assumptions about me only to be brought short when someone else mentioned reading my piece in a fancy journal or congratulated me on a fellowship. Their awkward embarrassment was their own fault and they were in the wrong and it made me happy. But these days I'm trying to be less smug in these situations, since my eagerness to show them up and show off means I'm colluding in the disdain of the dabbler.

And the concept of "dabbler" as a negative has become suspect to me. The poet and essayist Michele Sharpe calls dabblers the anticapitalists of the writing world. Being lost in the creative moment has value for a person and for society no matter the results. Exploring the craft tools of writing has value no matter the intention, talent, or time spent. The word "dabbler" could be stripped of judgment and become a simple description. Still, it would be inaccurate to label me a dabbler at this point. There are words I've reclaimed with exuberance—"dyke," "gimp," "hag," "fat." "Dabbler" can't be one of them. My moments of creative joy now come from composing a well-worked sentence or when I solve the puzzle of a structure or wake from a dream that gives me the perfect phrase. The old, original thrill that came from the act of putting words on paper and had less to do with the quality of that work is gone. Sometimes I miss it.

Alligator snapping turtles hunt at night in rivers near my house. They weigh two hundred pounds and can bite with the force of a thousand pounds but mostly don't attack. They prefer the more efficient life of choosing a likely place and lying in wait for curious fish with their jaws spread, unmoving except for the fleshy, bright pink tentacle that wiggles up from their tongues. It's called a lingual lure. At seventy, they and I are coming up on the end stage of our lifespans.

A grant asked how I saw my writing career developing in the next ten years. The question made me laugh. I think they had a younger applicant in mind and didn't know they were asking me what I wanted to get done before I died. But it's a good question, nevertheless. A decade is an arbitrary number of years to choose but a helpful one. With disability there has always been the honing down of what is possible to what is most important. It has always given me a clarity and self-governance. With age, a similar focus is required. For the grant application I made a list: complete a second collection of essays, prepare a manuscript of short stories, and write another novel. But then I wondered how long I will continue to strive in the same unrelenting way. And what it means about legacy and purpose if I stop. And I'm curious about what will emerge to the forefront if I clear the space to become my version of an old lady dabbler. These are the questions that will have the most exciting answers.

Turritopsis dohrnii is a jellyfish found in Florida waters. Under stress it will rebirth itself and thus is considered biologically immortal. But I more often consider the live oak tree arching over our house that might be three hundred years old. The trunk shows no signs of heart rot, but the branches fall from time to time. The big ones are called widow-makers. I hope its lifespan surpasses mine, and I'm able to forgo that particular grieving. But perhaps we'll pass on together, the tree and I, each of us having trimmed away the superfluous.

THE BEGINNING AND THE END

My mother is drowning. The hospice doctor sits on the bed with her, face to face, her soft tones murmuring in response to my mother's quaver of an English accent, which has become stronger. This must have been the way she spoke to me as I was born, the first words I heard, before the years in the United States changed her. I watch them from the side. One profile is perched high over a neck, the other sinks into hunched shoulders.

"What is happening to me?" My mother's question has been exhaled on breath that has become the sound of a child making bubbles in her milk with a straw.

I close my eyes. I am not breathing at all. How do they answer here at hospice when the question is asked?

"What do you think is happening?" the doctor says.

I look again. My mother's eye, the one I can see, is lost in an exhaustion of wrinkles. It slits open, and her head lifts enough that I can see the quiver of her chin. She stares at the doctor. No words. No words. We wait. Is she scared to die? Is she more scared that someone will say the words?

The doctor holds her hand and leans until their foreheads almost touch. My mother's billowing curtain of an eyelid drops. She sucks a breath into liquid lungs, and her body falls into itself once again.

There's a picture of my mother right after the war, 1948 perhaps. She has lived through the Blitz of London. In the photograph she stands on a beach in France, breasts out, legs poised, and the wind blows through her mass of black hair. Ocean waves curl at her feet. She's wearing one of the first bikinis.

"Let's give you something to make you more comfortable, shall we?" The doctor says this in the kindest voice I've ever heard. We have spoken of this moment when the distress of drowning will override the dangers of medicating.

My mother will not speak again. And now I am choking. And now the morphined end of things will begin.

DAY THIRTY-FIVE

On September 7, 1940, a twenty-mile swath of bombers and their accompanying fighters flew from Germany, over the English Channel, and on to London. The nine hundred and sixty-five planes bombed the city. The raids continued for fifty-seven consecutive days. One million bombs were dropped.

Jostled by neighbors carrying blankets and children and suitcases of precious things, Lena and Yvonne climb the concrete steps. They have spent the night in the tube station. Mother and daughter, arm in arm, they rise toward the gray light above them. They pause at the top. A snow of ash, cotton ticking, and feathers tumbles through the air and, mixed with fog and the scent of burnt asphalt, clings to their sweaters. Somewhere there is fire. Somewhere close there will be a home whose mattresses and pillows have been exploded out of windows. A siren signals the all clear.

Yvonne rushes ahead of her mother, and her gait is a fourteen-year-old mixture of languid woman and bony-kneed gallop. Lena calls her daughter back to her side and teaches by example the brisk walk that is just as fast but gives no outward sign of panic. They move through the debris on the narrow streets, through the crowds of tired people all doing their own brisk walks, all not quite breathing until they reach the corner that will give them the first view of their own homes. Before Lena and Yvonne arrive at theirs, a man in a steel helmet intercepts them. It wasn't ours. Bernard says this close to the ears of his wife and daughter. He walks a little way with them and tells light-hearted stories about his night watch, about helping a dog give birth, about the dotty old woman who left her curtains open again. I'm going to have a cup of tea at the warden post. I'll be home to change for work. Lena and Yvonne watch him disappear into a cloud of smoke.

They turn their corner and get the first glimpse. Each house in the row is still attached to the one beside it, and not a single grime-stained brick is thrown into the street. No windows are shattered onto the rose beds underneath them. Lena and Yvonne have developed a routine. Yvonne goes through the house by feel, past the still-blacked-out windows, to the bathroom in the back garden. Lena stokes the stove and fills a pot for tea. She sets out three precious eggs to boil and slices the hard end of a loaf. They pass in the hall. Yvonne goes up the narrow stairs to her bedroom, where she pulls back the drapes and dresses for school in the thin light. Soon she hears her mother climb the stairs, humming, ready to change into overalls for her factory job. Yvonne is in front of the mirror, trying out a new hairstyle, when her mother screams. She rushes to her parents' bedroom, a brush still gripped in one hand.

It's too light, is her first thought. Then she sees the hole in the roof over the bed and goes to her mother and touches her arm. Lena isn't staring at the ceiling. Yvonne follows her gaze to the bed, and the brush drops from her hand. They both jerk as it hits and then bounces twice on the floorboards but don't look away from the bed. The eiderdown comforter is piled high at the edges, almost covering the deep indentation in its center. Lena leans over the bed, putting one hand on her daughter's chest to push her back. She sees a length of metallic gray, fat in the middle and tapered to fins at the end—the bomb is a parody of a person sleeping. They bend together to look under the bed. The slats are broken and the mattress is pushed to within an inch of the floor.

Darling, run. Find your father. Lena whispers to her daughter without turning. Yvonne bursts into the street and ignores the concern of the neighbors as she runs to where her father finishes up his shift. His team are spread out over chairs, yawning, naming the stores they saw looted the night before. Yvonne falls at Bernard's feet, causing tea to slosh into its saucer. He and his shift listen to her breathless story, and the men have collected their gear before she finishes. Yvonne leaves before Bernard can stop her. She stays ahead of the men and calls to her mother as she reaches the still-open door. She runs lightly up the stairs. Lena has not moved. Yvonne takes her by the hand and turns them away from the ersatz sleeper. Lena and Yvonne both take things as they leave the house. Lena, her husband's medals from the Great War that lie next to the washstand and a tintype of her own mother that hangs on the wall of the stairway. Yvonne, a music box topped with a couple dancing that sits on the entryway table and her favorite hat from the coatrack by the door.

Bernard and his men pass them at the door. He points wordlessly up the street. Lena and Yvonne walk to the first corner before they stop and turn. Their neighbors evacuate their own homes and gather around. They are silent, except for the one that can never be quiet. The never-quiet man's voice blurs around them and their collective annoyance with him comforts and bonds them. Then they hear laughing and the tail end of a tasteless joke. Pushing through the doorway, too many at once, the men swagger into the street. Four of them bear a weighted sling out the door and into a panel truck. Bernard shakes hands all around and waves to his family. It's all over, come back.

Lena and Yvonne and Bernard sit at their kitchen table. The teakettle is steaming. The medals, the picture, the hat, and the music box are scattered over the table between the bread plate and the soft-boiled eggs waiting in their cups. Bernard slices off the top off his with one neat stroke of the knife. Yvonne turns the key under the music box and the couple turns this way and that. Lena sings the words to the tune. Pack up all my cares and woe, here I go, singing low. Yvonne and Bernard join her for the chorus. Bye-bye black-bird, bye-bye.

This story of a bomb in my grandparent's bed is, as are most family stories, truth embellished with fiction on the narrator's, my mother's, part. And I've added much invention of my own. My mother told the story with an emphasis on the bomb. But I am distanced from her experience of fear in the night and passing by daily destruction. For me the story is about emerging.

We watch emergings on television. The aerial views of students stumbling away from a building with their hands behind their heads. A reporter tripping among debris to interview survivors of a tornado as they pick through remains for something, anything. Our held breaths as we count the running, hunched-over figures escaping from a synagogue. The huddles of despair as we wait too long for the survivors of the shooting at a gay bar to appear.

World War II London had an etiquette for the mornings after a night of bombing. The unspoken rules were don't run or push, don't shout your relief or thank god when you find your home intact, don't collapse in wailing grief if it isn't. These behaviors were deemed unseemly and inconsiderate of other people in their own possible suffering. Even seventy years later my mother had disdain for people not "handling" themselves during a crisis. But when the nightly news hour would broadcast bombings from Vietnam all the way to Iraq years later, she would go to the kitchen, pour a drink, light another cigarette, and fry slices of Spam. It had been welcome protein during the long years of rationing. It comforted her.

In the United States we are mostly the ones who bomb. But still, our "mornings after" are increasing, what with frequent climate change–induced disasters and so many mass shootings that the media now picks and chooses which ones to report on. Many communities and people know we will be considered last, if ever, because of racism, geographic remoteness, or age and disability. We've known this for a while. We've come to understand that first responders are not the police, fire fighters, or even the paramedics. We who are emerging are the first responders. What can we learn from each other? Can we collaborate? How do we develop an etiquette of useful compassion?

I SAY MY NAME

January 2018

My beloved and I fight about politics. Not about our politics but that her grief means she needs to talk about every egregious tweet, and I can't bear to hear his name. It's a relief when I sleep late, Pam leaves for work, and I avoid the report from her morning scrolling. We work together on local elections, which is the only politics that makes sense to me anymore.

I take a friend for a colonoscopy and take a friend to physical therapy after his hip replacement. I bring a meal to Fred, who is trapped in a nursing home. We're not really friends but have been part of the same local queer community for over a quarter of a century. He uses a wheelchair like me and has a pressure sore that won't heal. This is the stuff of nightmares for me. More for him, I remind myself as I cry with relief after every visit, relief that I get to leave. At the memorial service of one of our old lesbians, the widow's face breaks me apart.

Corporations thrive within this terrible new order of things. Pam's company takes their employees to Las Vegas for surpassing yearly goals. Wives are included. Why not, we decide. I've never been on a corporate trip. Among conservative heads of industry, there isn't a whiff of homophobia that we care to notice. The company pays for a Cirque de Soleil show, my first, and I almost throw myself over the balcony in wonder and alarm with each dive and leap. The company has a party where people eat, drink, and hit golf balls from elevated bays that overlook the lights of the city. I give money to women decked out in headdresses, spangled leotards, and a spray of feathers attached to their rear ends so they'll pose with Pam. Everything is extravagant and extreme and ridiculous. Pam and I play and make love and laugh. We take the bonus cash given to us for gambling and rent a wheelchair accessible van and drive through Red Rock Canyon. By this time, the silence is a balm.

February

I use the NEA grant money to hire a publicist, Jeremy, for the memoir that launches in September. I reason that I'll be sixty-six, the future is always unknown, and this book deserves the best chance I can give it. He doesn't ask directly but he did read the memoir so he must have questions about disability and stamina. I have no limits, I tell him, except that sometimes I have to pace by adding extra time to travel schedules. We make plans.

Soon after that he says he's moving from New York to Barcelona to be with his beloved and newborn baby. Do I still want to work with him? I decide that most everything these days can be done from anywhere. And who would I be not to make "reasonable accommodations"?

We jump out of our kayaks to swim in the springs of the Chassahowitzka River. It's a warm winter day in Florida and spring water is always a steady seventy-two degrees.

All of us friends take photos of each other underwater, in the clear water, our clothes billowing, and our hair spread as if we are floating in air except for the bubbles rising up off our limbs.

March

Aliesa and I take one of our "the poet and the prose writer hit the road" road trips to a writers' conference. On the way, she plans the menu for the book's local launch party, six months away. In the midst of fourteen thousand attendees, I revel in the experience that, for the first time, because of the grant and the book coming out, when asked "What's up these days?" I have something to say that's considered noteworthy. I meet the writer I've been mentoring online. Sarah and I, collaborators and friends, organize a reading of the contributors to *Older Queer Voices*, an anthology we edited. It was a response to our mutual despair after the presidential election. I make introductions and then retreat to the side of the room and listen to their stories of survival that remind us that survival is possible. Their voices put me in a liminal space that's about hope.

All of us campaign volunteers at the election party become quiet in waves as "She's getting the concession call" is whispered around the room. We watch her face, almost hear the murmur of her polite words. When she hangs up, we have the first African American woman, a progressive woman, from our district elected to the city council. By a landslide. This is repeated around the country.

Our town has one of the "March for Our Lives" protests. Pam makes signs. I scout the route for obstacles before I join her at the rally. It's best to anticipate them before I have to turn around in a thick group of protesters and clip ankles and push through waists, breasts, and crotches. I find a place I'll have to detour and memorize the cross street just before it so I can dart into the road for a block. I tell the organizers they need to announce the location of the obstacle before we start. They don't, and as I race in the street, I see another person, using a manual wheelchair, being lifted over the patch of ripped-up sidewalk. The people crowded around him are happy with the sudden camaraderie his need has given them. His hands grip the armrests and his face is a grimace. I'd rather be out here slipping though the traffic.

April

Page proofs of the memoir arrive from the publisher.

I visit Fred weekly. He now has an infection in the wound. He will be on antibiotics forever. At some point the last of them will fail. I don't know what to do with the hopelessness. He talks about planning to visit the Taj Mahal. The writer I'm working with and I have another of our mentoring calls. In situations where I would be harsh and full of self-reproach, she writes with such tenderness for herself and others. I try to imagine writing this way. Pam and I attend another old lesbian's memorial service, where another widow is in a daze while thanking us for our condolences.

Jeremy sends on the official invitations to the Miami Book Fair and the Southern Festival of the Book in Nashville along with a batch of interview requests. But the first live event is planned for the Decatur Book Festival near Atlanta on the actual day of the book release. I used to live in Decatur. Scenes from my memoir are set in the official bookstore of the festival. The high school I graduated from, also mentioned in the memoir, is up the road. Four years ago, because of all these connections, I naively thought I was a shoo-in, but the festival committee rejected me and my debut novel. I was told the novel's publisher wasn't established enough for them. Perhaps I shouldn't, perhaps I should stay in solidarity with those of us who have published with small presses, but the truth is that, today, I feel triumphant in all the ways. I strived. I won. I celebrate.

May

More opportunities arrive from Jeremy. My hair carries home the industrial cleaning smell of lemon-tinted chlorine after another visit with Fred, and I decide to get my own life and body in the best possible state as a form of book-launch prep. I set up routine appointments: dentist, haircut, get the crack in the car's windshield repaired, mammogram, the dog's yearly physical, acupuncture, have the van's power seat and ramp serviced, and AC unit maintenance.

The press's fall/winter catalog arrives. On page twenty-four is my book. They can't change their minds now despite the times I wake up from dreams where they have.

The dental checkup goes well.

I review the workshop manuscripts for an upcoming conference where I have a fellowship.

It becomes known that parents and children are being separated at the border. Hundreds of them, including infants and toddlers, are under five. I am distraught. I was hospitalized, over and over, from eight months old until I was five. It was in a time when parents were allowed a single half-hour visit a day. For many months, I was in a hospital hundreds of miles from my family. I was sometimes in a ward lined with beds, but I always had a bed. Sometimes I lay in sheets pooled with urine, but only briefly. And I was never in a cage with professionally cruel men guarding me. I was never an "alien." My anguish was never without moments of kindness. All I can think to do is send money.

I remember not to put on deodorant before today's mammogram appointment.

They say not to worry, but I need a second mammogram. A friend is in town to give a writing craft talk. We have a visit after. I don't mention the mammogram. It's the last week of the mentorship, and I and the kind writer make our goodbyes. I don't mention the mammogram. I send the corrected page proofs back to the publisher. The memoir is now available online for reviewers. The follow-up mammogram shows two masses. A biopsy can't be scheduled for twelve days.

The air smells different, crisper each time I drive over a river on the way to the Panhandle: the Santa Fe, Ichetucknee, Suwannee, Fenholloway, Ecofina, Aucilla, St. Marks, and Wakulla. I take a route that hugs the coast so I can visit the small creatures living in the aquarium at Panacea, the home of Jack Rudloe, whose nature writing inspired mine. The Sopchoppy and Ochlockonee Rivers smell of high-tide salt. I've decided not to cancel going to the conference. What is the other choice—stay home, wait, worry, be afraid, feel Pam's fear? And no one at the conference will know that I'm in the in-between. In-between the knowing looks and careful kindness of the mammogram staff and the actual knowing.

The beach, with no ramp, is a focus of the conference. Special lounge chairs are set out above the surf just for participants. Drinks are served there at sunset. I know all this because people share photos that I see on social media. In one, a group of them make funny faces from behind a sandcastle and a hemorrhage of rage bursts over me. There, alone, in my small bed, it cracks open all the other angers—the chronic, lifelong anger of being left out, the last election, the children in cages, and finally the hot, exploding core of wrathful fury that I might have cancer.

All week I know I'm a coward not to make a scene. And I'm letting down any other disabled writer who might want to attend. But I have lost perspective. If I say even one word, it will let loose a violent sobbing that I worry will never end and will mostly be about maybe having cancer. It's all I can do to not cry during the workshops, at meals, on the day of the anniversary of my mother's death, or going for ice cream with other writers. Not crying has become my goal. I wait to see if there are changes to the final blowout party that is usually on the beach around a bonfire. There aren't. I collude along with everyone else in ignoring the obvious. Instead, I leave the day before the party. I am alone. I am defeated. I'm so glad to be driving home over the rivers, to Pam and to my little dog.

The biopsy happens. And now it's a worse time of in-between. I fit in a visit to Fred and he barely speaks. I imagine him lost in his own silent anger. I tell him why I might not be back soon. The freedom I feel as I leave the nursing home for what might be a long stretch is from cowardice. I arrange for Pam and I go to the Florida Folk Festival, so Pam can listen to music all day. She's happy. I follow her from stage to stage, find shade to sit in, and watch her clap and hum along and I'm happy. I'm trying to get ahead of what might become, for the first time, despite what the world assumes about us, an imbalance of caretaking in our relationship.

———————

After what will never be a funny mix-up of missed calls because my phone is unexplainably set to silent, my primary care's office nurse tells me to wait, she'll get the doctor to the phone right away. Her eagerness to please is terrible. Pam is with me, both physically beside me and close with her love. Aliesa has dropped by to deliver her old dog for us to take care of while she and Kathy are gone. She is with me as well. The doctor's voice is gentle. Compassion has come to mean bad news. Invasive lobular carcinoma.

June

June 5: The surgeon says a lumpectomy and radiation and that should be that. I know it's best to personalize myself with medical people, so I tell her about the book launch and ask if I'll be good to go by September. She counts backward on a calendar. She offers to do surgery tomorrow. She uses her surgeon authority to clear the way for us to get all the pre-op chores done today. I look at Pam. She nods. And we're off in a flurry of blood draws, EKGs, and form filling. We arrive home exhausted. I do the first of three antiseptic scrubs of my breasts I have to complete by the next day.

Then I cancel my birthday party for two days later. Which means saying the word "cancer" over and over. Also, it seems time to let Jeremy in on what's happening. He responds, "You can focus on getting better, and I'll take care of the book." I fall in love with him a little.

June 6: The only times we've ever used the van's wheelchair tie-down straps in the back have been to pick up Aliesa's mother for dinner, to take Pam's mother to appointments, to bring our friend Jessie to parties at our house or the time Pam brought her home from the hospital after she had her baby. Coming home from the lumpectomy, we fit the straps to my wheelchair for the first time. I don't like it. And I'm in pain. And it's been a quarter century since I've sat in the back of a car, so I didn't remember that it makes me nauseated.

A box of advanced reader's copies of the memoir is waiting at the front door when we arrive home. Among all the advice offered by the breast cancer community that has gathered around me, ice packs are emphasized. I'm hovering one over the wound, experimenting with the right amount of pressure to avoid pain yet get the most from the cold, while Pam opens the box. The bitterness of iodine spreading up from the bandages is replaced by the slick, acetate smell of new books. The cover is perfect. The size is perfect. The typeface is perfect.

June 7: My sixty-sixth birthday. I spend it in bed with my dog curled between my legs and with Pam hovering and let a wash of social media celebrate me. Sarah, from her worried geographical distance, sends the gift of a social media advertising campaign for the memoir. Aliesa has informed me in her outraged voice that I can cancel my party but one cannot cancel cake. So, I know she and Kathy will be over. In the afternoon, Pam helps me slide into my wheelchair, and she and the little dog escort me on a slow, careful stroll around the neighborhood. When we come back around the final corner, I find that one cannot cancel a party either. Friends, Beckie, Madeline, Taylor, Lee, the ones of twenty and thirty years, the ones who don't care what I think I need, who know they have a right to be part of my life, to show up no matter what I say, have arms full of flowers and gaudily wrapped packages and crowd the driveway waiting to be let in. The cake bearers arrive as well. I get back under the covers. They fit chairs into the small bedroom and some sit gently on the bed. They exclaim and cry over copies of the book, they eat cake, and they climb over each other to switch out ice packs for me.

Facebook tells me that a year ago we were kayaking in Alaska, in Aialik Bay. I remember the frenzy of bubbles as humpback whales circled underwater, corralling fish into a pack, and then lunging up through them, mouths wide. I remember killer whales. I remember porpoises and puffins. The small icebergs around us snapped and crackled as they melted and we inhaled oxygen from twenty-three thousand years ago. I remember watching, from a half mile away, a ledge of ice split off the glacier. We had to wait for the sound of it to reach us. We had to wait even longer to feel the rise of water.

Pam suggests an excursion to our Sweetwater Wetlands, with its flat paths, where the lotus are blooming, tall and golden. The summer heat bakes into my shoulders.

June 20: A second lumpectomy. The first one didn't have "clean margins." Which means radiation is delayed. Pam is out of town for work, but I tell her we know the drill, no need to come back, it's just another day surgery, she'll be home the next day, and Aliesa will take me and take care of me. Before we leave for the hospital, I send Jeremy my responses for an interview he arranged. On the way home Aliesa teaches me, from her long experience, how to lessen nausea on car rides. Staring into the far horizon is helpful.

I am distraught that Pam isn't here. It shocks me that I'm distraught. I sob for her. Pam texts and calls before the first flight, during the layover, deboarding after the second flight, even on the five-mile drive home from the airport. Just a month ago, this would have annoyed me. But something shifts between us, something about who we are to each other and about death and something about love.

I lift myself up toward the edge of the bathtub like always and fall back into the water. I'm disbelieving of the situation and try again and again, each time with less success. The water gets cold. I reheat it. Aliesa, who is over to check on things, who is in the kitchen preparing the meal she brought, calls out to ask if I'm all right. I'm not. She brings me a step stool to put in the tub. She helps lift my legs. We joke about our new level of intimacy. Later, she brings me more ice packs. Later, Pam and I tell each other this loss was to be expected and is temporary. She digs through the closet for the bath seat I use when we're camping and sets it up.

The nausea persists. I can only eat yoghurt, ice cream, and Kathy's mashed potatoes, which she delivers regularly. A local glossy publishes an excerpt from the memoir.

Jeremy sends a list of fancier-than-I-had-expected places that are interested in essays and excerpts prelaunch. He submits the book for awards. He asks, since the start of radiation is now delayed, if I'll be able to travel so soon after it ends. I tell him no problem and that we are still on schedule for all our plans.

They say it's important that I don't cancel the physical therapy appointment. Avoiding lymphedema is important, they insist. When I get there, it seems most important that they can do all the measurements needed for their long-term study. But I am glad I forced myself up and out of the house.

I drive the car on my own to have the seat motor serviced. The car needs to work for my book launch plans to succeed. I visit the chiropractor for the first time since all this began. I shop for groceries. It's a weird ecstasy to be doing errands again.

Jeremy suggests that we can be more selective with the in-person events. That I can be reading from the book a year from now. "It doesn't have to be a sprint out of the gate with the stress of the commitments at an uncertain time." Instead of my usual taking offense when someone thinks I can't do something, I'm relieved to the point of crying.

The last surgery results are "clean margins." Radiation begins soon. I know it isn't how this disease works, but I am declaring myself technically cancer free.

I have moments of less nausea. Sometimes the food friends bring me tastes good. I watch Hannah Gadsby's special three times. If you live in the margins, "self-deprecating humor is not humility. It's humiliation." The nausea returns. I spend more time in bed. On Alaska's live bear cam, I watch a mother suddenly hurry her cubs out of the water and into the brush. Minutes later a male, massive, bigger than all the other males, plods into view. The mother must have smelled him coming. She reappears and now looks like a bear in miniature, a dollhouse bear, in comparison. But she faces the male with her legs bowed wide. Neither of them moves. Then the male turns and goes into the water to fish. The cubs reappear. Word comes that some of the seized children are in a facility an hour from our house. This is a chance to show up. I don't go. I have to admit that it's physically not possible.

June 30: I'm drooling over the toilet and waiting to throw up again. What has felt like heartburn is now a stabbing pain through to my back. It's the worst pain I've ever felt. It is a different pain than I've ever felt. As I pant, I think of a fellow Florida outdoorswoman. She paddled the entire length of the St. Johns River. And she and her husband married later in life the same as Pam and I did. When we kayaked together, she told the story of her wedding day. As she was changing from her ceremony dress to her reception dress, she felt not terrible, but bad in a way she never had before. A friend, a nurse, took her to a nearby fire station. She was having a heart attack. I ask Pam to drive me to the emergency room.

I'm hospitalized with a heart attack. They can't do a cardiac catheterization right away because for some as yet unknown reason I've had too much blood loss in the past month. The lumpectomies do not explain it.

Pam sets up a remote work office in the corner of the hospital room. I'm given blood until my hemoglobin reaches the permitted level, not within normal limits, but good enough to allow the catheterization.

July

July 1: On the large screen my spine looks like the trunk of a palm tree. I can see my heart beating. I ask questions about anatomy and the nurse by my head points out physical landmarks to me like discs and the bulge that is a ventricle. A tube winds into view, squirts a liquid, and my arteries flash over my heart like heat lightning through clouds. She points out a thick sideways artery. That's called the widow-maker, she ways. A clot there is serious. She points out the narrowed area in another artery, which is where my problem is. The room is in twilight and the movements in the room are a dance. The many voices are steady and overlap in a practiced way. Then the nurse at my head jerks away. The voices become clipped and impatient with each other. I see a small darkness move through the widow-maker artery. The tube chases it, spraying it over and over. Voices raise, but the words "a clot" are whispered. The nurse is back. She slides her hand under my gown and slaps sticky paddle-shaped pads on my torso. "Just a precaution," she says in a thin voice. She hisses to the doctor that I'm alert, and he needs to tell me what's going on. "My chest hurts the same it did when I was having the heart attack," I say. My thoughts blur as a narcotic is hurried into the IV. When I come to, Pam's eyes, the pupils mostly, fill my field of view. I turn my head and throw up.

Jeremy says he's heard from the *New York Times* editor who's interested in seeing a pitch. "Can you send me the essay about aging with disability when it's ready?" I read the email from my hospital bed and can only laugh.

I'm released. Strapped in the back of the van again, I pant through my mouth and stare at the horizon the way Aliesa taught me, but still I'm nauseated.

Once I'm propped up in my own bed by my own pillows, I reply to Jeremy. "That's good news about the NYT. Yes, I'll get the essay to you in a timely fashion. And the 'Withered Legs' piece is almost ready for the *Paris Review*. And this sounds like a bad joke when I say it, but I just had a minor heart attack. Aren't I a joy of a client?"

Frida is here with us while Aliesa and Kathy are out of town. She's a meatloaf of a little dog, toothless, mostly blind, and hard of hearing. She's happiest when dominating her world, which she does wherever she is. My dog, Pippin, tolerates her. I aspire to be her.

I have three medical appointments this week. My medical doctor is out of town but the office calls to check on me. They have me come in because of the fever. I tell the resident who've I've never met that something is terribly wrong but I don't have any specifics. I just feel really bad. He and his boss give me the old lady treatment and send me home without any tests.

The next appointment is a routine follow-up with the surgeon. We both stare at my breast. Just a hematoma, she says again. Which I know is bullshit. Maybe admitting it's an infection makes her stats look bad. But it seems more pressing that I tell her something is wrong, really wrong with me, but again I can't come up with a specific. She says call in two days if I'm not better. It feels like another old lady brush-off. I call two days later. Her office never responds. Frida yelps when we touch her. We call her vet, who makes a home visit and says she's strained her neck but give her baby aspirin and she'll be okay. A reviewer wants to know the name of the space archeologist mentioned in my memoir. I can't remember. Plus, what does it matter? Plus, I can't remember anything much. Jeremy says there are rumors of a *Kirkus* review. An essay, with changes, is returned by an editor.

The third appointment that week is a post–heart attack follow-up. I tell the cardiologist, whom I've never met before, how bad I'm feeling. She pays attention. She orders lab work and a chest X-ray. Says she'll be in touch as soon as the results are in. I believe her. She believed me. Which has me crying all the way home.

That evening I can't seem to get out of bed. I can't sit up in bed. The strength of my arms, of everywhere, is diminished. Pam has to pull me up. Help me transfer. She sets up a sponge bath. I tell Pam that it's as if the spirit is falling out of my body. Pam props me up on pillows. The snoring of old dogs surrounds me with comfort. I get on my laptop and give out money over and over. Is rampant donating a sign? Of what?

———

I'm in the bathroom again, scared again. It's 3 a.m. I transfer in and out of my wheelchair seat to the toilet, sometimes not able to swing the two inches between them as I take turns throwing up and having diarrhea. There's no chest pain. It's not like that, not like the heart attack. It's as if my muscles have collapsed into something less than weakness, into not being muscles anymore, into hollow spaces under my skin. My thoughts have become simple in a similar way. I slide, spreading feces over the seats, back into my wheelchair. Bent over to vomit again, I've forgotten to flush and this time see a bowl filled with blood. Fresh, bright blood swirling over black, thick shit. The smell jerks my head up. Like a foul version of smelling salts, it pulls me from the stupor and I make it back to the bedroom. I throw myself over the bed face down and butt up and wake Pam and ask her to clean me and the wheelchair. I decide I'll go to the ER as soon as I'm presentable and don't reek. Putting together the words needed to tell Pam the plan is beyond what I can do. I pass out. When I come to, light filters through the bedroom curtains, and the smell is gone. Pam must have cleaned everything. I think about my mother, who learned from the other ladies at her retirement home to always call an ambulance because that way you skip the waiting room and are taken directly into an ER cubical. But I just can't. It seems overly dramatic. And I'm not vomiting or having diarrhea anymore. And it would alert our neighbors, who are already worried about me. I don't want to be a spectacle. Pam helps me turn over and supports my back as I sit up. She hovers as I successfully slide into the wheelchair. I feel accomplished. She straps me down in the back of the van and drives me to the ER. I stare at the far horizon.

On the third day in the hospital, I lose the ability to make sense with my words. I know what I'm thinking, but no matter how hard I try, how much I concentrate, the words garble over each other in a nonsensical order. It pisses me off. It terrifies Pam. She calls out for a nurse and now I'm pissed at her. She's narcing on me. They are going to think I'm senile. They're going to use it to take away my right to make my own choices. I've never been so angry at Pam. This is a betrayal. Interns come in and do all the follow-my-eyes, squeeze-my-fingers tests and I'm fine. They reassure Pam that this sort of thing happens and I'll improve soon. She refuses to accept that and follows them out into the hall where I can't hear what is said. I've asked her never to do that. More betrayal. Soon I can speak clearly again, but anger and loss of trust is lodged in my body. I know it's not fair. Pam did the right thing to say something. I could have been having a stroke.

Jeremy sends me the *Kirkus* review. It's a good one. Except for the "stricken with polio-borne limitations" header. But I've already decided to be thrilled by each review best I can and to ignore, the best I can, all the inevitable "strickens," "sufferings," "braves," and "inspirings."

I leave the hospital five days later after more bags of blood, more tests, and the diagnosis of an ulcer and a postoperative breast abscess. I've had to cancel the radiation and medical oncologist appointments from my hospital bed. Another delay in moving forward. Jeremy emails that the finished books have arrived for him to send out to reviewers.

A physical therapist, Hector, comes to my home. We talk about his favorite Argentinian writers as he designs a program to strengthen my body. This time, I'm not bouncing back or pushing through or being sturdy or triumphant or rugged or stalwart or unbroken. I am broken. Every time—and it's often—someone says I'm "such a trooper," I yell at them. I hate the implied admiration when all I'm doing is surviving—so far. And I hate that image of a gear burdened, weaponed, tool-of-the-colonizer soldier trudging through a jungle. Friends tease me by warning each other, in front of me, "Watch out, don't say the "T" word," as they water my plants, tell funny stories, fold laundry, and switch out their casserole dishes with the next offering. Jeremy sets up podcasts, interviews, columns—anything I can do from my bed. Answering over email works better than podcasts since I'm still a slower thinker. I ask Jeremy to not be shy about reminding me about anything.

The radiation oncologist thinks the infection is healing from inside and we should go ahead and start radiation. Statistically, for the best results, it's already almost too long since surgery.

The *Paris Review* editor sends edits. "Do you think you could send me a version with your edits/approvals by Wednesday evening?" It's Monday.

The medical oncologist is all about statistics. He enters my information and pulls up tables that deduce my percentage of survival from the massive, long-term studies of breast cancer patients in England and Sweden, places there are socialized medicine. All I can remember is the number 8 percent. But I don't remember percent of what. He says I'll most likely die of something else, not breast cancer. Not to worry.

With the triumph of a marathoner, I get in and out of the damn bathtub by myself.

August

Jeremy passes on more requests for essays. One is a request for a piece on feminist science fiction from the 1970s, which means I get to pull out my precious, crumbling, yellowed paperbacks that make me sneeze and write about them and take photos of the original covers. By the time I've bent over, again and again, in front of my bookshelves, I'm exhausted. And happy.

A writer friend and I spend a Sunday afternoon trading emails back and forth to create what will become a conversation about the memoir for the *L.A. Review of Books*. We have fun together. I make bad jokes. I'm mentally confident. This is the moment I know I'll become myself again. It makes me giddy.

The bad jokes continue. I sign off "warmly" on all my emails to Jeremy during the terrible heat wave in Barcelona. He answers with a photo of the view outside his second-floor office window—a partially constructed giant paper-mâché bust of Julius Caesar stares in at him.

The twenty-six days of radiation begins. The staff becomes concerned that I don't have anyone with me. One of them is sniffy about "Where's my wife?" I don't owe them an explanation. I don't tell them I won't let Pam come, except for that once to show her the situation. I don't tell them that this is the first time I've been able to be on my own in too long. That after the treatment, I go somewhere, anywhere, for a bagel, to buy a fancy cheese, to browse in a bookstore, and no one knows where I am. These are luxurious moments. I continue not to visit Fred. It's as if I don't have enough fortitude to spare.

Radiation has turned my skin a blaze of red. Pain pounds at my breast fifty times a day. I assure myself and everyone else that the original schedule is delayed enough that I won't have time to develop any of the really bad effects like exhaustion until after the trip to Decatur, if ever.

Pus bubbles from an opening in the surgical scar. It stains my bras. I buy sterile pads and slip one into the cup, but it slides around so I tape the pad in place. It's just paper tape, hardly sticky at all, but it's a mistake. I stare down past my nose to my breast and have a close-up view as the skin under the tape dissolves into what looks like a cherry slushie. Clumps of it stick to the tape as I hurry to remove it. I press the tip of a finger around my breast, exploring. Each tap threatens any cohesiveness that remains in the skin, like a skim of ice over a lake.

My hemoglobin isn't perfect yet. The hematologist suggests an iron infusion. I nix it. I point out that my levels are improving. We should just wait. Mostly I say no because it's too close to book launch. I don't say this out loud to anyone because it makes me seem psychologically suspect. But I can't risk a reaction.

I'm strong. I get a haircut. I scrub the drip pan in the toaster oven and hand-wash a silk shawl and a silk shirt. I put on earrings and a cute hat before I go to another physical therapy appointment. They say it's a sign when one begins to accessorize again. I bring Fred meatloaf from a deli counter. He's back from a hospital stay because of kidney problems from the newest antibiotic. He describes in great detail the hot nurse, a young Johnny Depp look-alike, and I go along with the mood although I'm not feeling it myself and mention the way-butch resident in the Radiation Department. We laugh. I cook dinner for Pam—pan-fried salmon over noodles with goat cheese, capers, and dill. I put together a proposal for readings from recently released memoirs for a writers' conference many, many months into the future.

Purple sprays of giant ironweed wave over my head, salt-and-pepper shrubs scratch against my arms, and I have to push through firebush blooms that droop across my path. Clematis vines wind through it all. Every August, the yard is overgrown the way I like it. Butterflies ignore me in their rush to reproduce. An eastern tiger swallowtail touches down on the flower pattern of my dress. They taste with their feet, and right away this one knows cotton isn't the place to lay eggs. It flits on in search of the next plant. I think about the milkweed in the front yard it might like. The butterfly dashes around my wheelchair and heads off in that direction.

Pam has continued to phone bank, fundraise, and hold signs on corners. Sometimes she says "we," and includes me in her efforts. I just let her. But all I really do is give dribs and drabs of money. The elections are a mix of anguish and hope. Locally, again, there is hope. We elect more African American women. But I remember the retaliation after 1991, when in response to the Clarence Thomas debacle, four women, including the first African American woman, were elected to the Senate. I brace.

The breast pain that used to beat on me strikes less. The tenderness continues, so I automatically set guards around it. My arm braces around my front at the approach of a hug. And in bed, lying on my side, which I can do now, I keep my elbow planted in front of my chest with my forearm raised in the air. It serves a similar function to the concrete bollards in front of federal buildings designed to deter car bombs. It is the bulwark against my beloved's sleeping shifts in position and our automatic reachings for each other in the night. Spooning has become a careful art. I have told her what hurts and what doesn't, and we have adapted.

And now all I'm thinking about is clothes. I need my first outfit since before. I don't like to dress as if I'm trying to hide my fat or my cleavage. But this outfit has to be gentle over the breast. I have a bright coral, swingy top. I have linen pants in a complimentary shade of peach. I have shiny silver shoes that lace up so they can be adjusted for swelling. I have a thin scarf festooned with strands of lace to drape over my chest. It's a blob-like look, but it's flamboyant and shiny. I've learned to tape the sterile pads to the bra rather than my skin. Pam helps me wipe the dust and debris off all the surfaces on my wheelchair. She listens to my reading and to the many versions of the "relaxed and genuine" introduction I've prepared and memorized. She tells me I am beautiful.

The poet and the prose writer are on the road to the Decatur Book Festival. Aliesa has come with me to the radiation appointment that morning, where the late-arriving clinic staff warns us that a massive wreck on the freeway has cars backed up throughout the town. As we successfully detour around the traffic, I joke that in the Russian roulette that is I-75, statistically, we've dodged the bullet. We reach the city limits, and I sing out that we've left cancer town behind. Aliesa lists all the places the book has been promoted, all the essays published, all the interviews, all the podcasts. I fake-humble protest but then start filling in the accomplishments she's left out. We discuss the best proportions of savory to sweet food for the local launch party later in the month. We reach the Georgia border, and I screech like a kid on a roller coaster. Cancer state is behind us.

Coming into Atlanta, the traffic tightens as the lanes multiply and narrow. Aliesa, the driver, stays unruffled as a car slides from the outside lane, close past the nose of our car, and bumps onto the shoulder. When a truck decides to ride the yellow line beside us and I slam my hand on the dashboard and make a shuddering gasp, she remains calm. By the time we've had to slow for two more wrecks, instinctively duck when a car speeds around and past us and continues an erratic race forward, and spend time enclosed front and back, side to side, by eighteen-wheelers, we decide we're inside a video game. We joke that, so far, our screen hasn't exploded into the words "You died."

We are finally off the freeway. It's two miles to the hotel when we hear the siren. It gets louder. We can see flashing just over the tops of cars in the distance. And then the traffic parts, lining up to either side of us, our lane clears, and an ambulance races head-on toward us, becoming large in the windshield. It never slows, but at the last moment finds a gap and is gone. The traffic forms around us again. For the first time, Aliesa has a hard time driving. Because we're laughing. We arrive at the hotel still choking. I have to pause just away from the lobby desk before I can breathe well enough to say my name. I say my name. I say I'm an author with the festival. I say I've arrived.

ACKNOWLEDGMENTS

Thank you to the *Sun Magazine*, the *New York Times*, the *Paris Review*, *New Letters*, the *Writer's Chronicle*, and *Sweet: A Literary Confection*, where versions of these essays have been previously published. And my Substack newsletter has provided a space for the development of essays such as "Writing while High" and "Old. Lady. Dabbler."

And, as always, thank you to Aliesa Zoecklein, Michele Sharpe, and the community of friends and writers who make my creative life possible. These essays in particular were encouraged and improved on by Sarah Einstein and Alex DiFrancesco as well as Aisha Sabatini Sloan, Min Li Chan, Tessa Fontaine, and the writings of the rest of our cohort at the 2021 Sewanee Writers' Conference.

In my sixties,
I found my beloved Pam who gives me adventures and daily laughter.
She makes everything possible.

Crux, the Georgia Series in Literary Nonfiction

JOHN GRISWOLD, *The Age of Clear Profit:
Collected Essays on Home and the Narrow Road*

JOSEPH GEHA, *Kitchen Arabic: How My Family Came
to America and the Recipes We Brought with Us*

LAWRENCE LENHART, *Backvalley Ferrets:
A Rewilding of the Colorado Plateau*

SARAH BETH CHILDERS, *Prodigals:
A Sister's Memoir of Appalachia*

JODI VARON, *Your Eyes Will Be My Window: Essays*

SANDRA GAIL LAMBERT, *My Withered Legs and Other Essays*